Brimming with creative inspiration, how-to projects, and useful information to enrich your everyday life, quarto.com is a favorite destination for those pursuing their interests and passions.

First Published in 2022 by Cool Springs Press,
an imprint of The Quarto Group,
100 Cummings Center, Suite 265-D,
Beverly, MA 01915, USA.
T (978) 282-9590 F (978) 283-2742
Quarto.com

Cool Springs Press titles are also available at discount for retail, wholesale, promotional, and bulk purchase. For details, contact the Special Sales Manager by email at specialsales@quarto.com or by mail at The Quarto Group, Attn: Special Sales Manager, 100 Cummings Center, Suite 265-D, Beverly, MA 01915, USA.

26 25 24 23 22 1 2 3 4 5

ISBN: 978-0-7603-7299-9

Digital edition published in 2022
eISBN: 978-0-7603-7300-2

Library of Congress Cataloging-in-Publication Data

Names: McEnaney, Ryan, author.
Title: Field guide to outside style : design and plant your perfect outdoor space / Ryan McEnaney.
Other titles: Design and plant your perfect outdoor space
Description: Beverly, MA, USA : Cool Springs Press, 2022. | Includes index.
Identifiers: LCCN 2022005690 (print) | LCCN 2022005691 (ebook) | ISBN 9780760372999 (board) | ISBN 9780760373002 (ebook)
Subjects: LCSH: Landscape design. | Landscape gardening. | Gardens—Designs and plans. | Handbooks and manuals.
Classification: LCC SB473 .M363 2022 (print) | LCC SB473 (ebook) | DDC 712/.6—dc23/eng /20220215
LC record available at https://lccn.loc.gov /2022005690
LC ebook record available at https://lccn.loc.gov /2022005691

Design and page layout: Laura Shaw Design
Cover photos credits:
Front top left: Adam Woodruff
Front top right: Tracy Walsh
Front bottom left: Tracy Walsh
Front bottom right: Joe Dodd, Linear Photography, Carson Douglas Landscape Architecture, Designer
Back cover: Shutterstock
Illustration: Lisa Nunamaker

Printed in China

FIELD GUIDE TO

Outside Style

Design & Plant Your Perfect Outdoor Space

RYAN McENANEY

COOL SPRINGS PRESS

Contents

Introduction

HI FRIENDS. Thanks so much for taking this journey with me. I'll start by letting you in on my background and why I should be giving any advice on designing your yard. The first thing you need to know is that I'm not a horticulturist. Now, don't let that make you shut the book and walk away. I grew up in the nursery business and have been working in it for a decade. But I say that so you know that I've been in your shoes. I came into the plant world with no real training or background and have learned everything by doing it. I've stared at a blank slate of dirt and wondered what the heck to do. I've seen the Latin names on plant tags and have been totally confused by the literal other language. So, I'm with you and I'll be your guide as you start to plan your outdoor space.

To me, creating this garden or landscape or outdoor room, or whatever you may call it, is not just a reflection of your personal style, but it is an extension of your home. It's a place that you get to create from scratch, make your own, and in which you can develop a great sense of pride. So, approaching this is a big deal. Not only because it's where you'll host friends and family for years to come, but also because it's a lot of physical work and financial input. I don't take it lightly, so that's why I ventured out to create this guide.

Coming home should be a joy. With help from these pages, your outdoor living space can become an extension of your home's interior and a reflection of your personal style, even if you don't consider yourself a gardener.

I wanted to develop something that everyone could be inspired by, get excited about digging in the dirt, and work to create a masterpiece that brings joy to their lives. Because at the end of the day, planting a garden is one of the most beautiful, albeit slow, forms of living art in the world.

Now, don't worry. I won't stay so "in the clouds" for the rest of this book. But it's important for you to know where I'm coming from as we start this partnership. Curating your outdoor space is an ongoing process. Setting up the initial structure and bones of the yard will give you a framework from which to work over the years. It's like the foundation of your house. If that's solid, you can move walls and change up the paint, but the house itself will stay in place. Bear with me through my (sometimes terrible) puns and analogies throughout the book. They may be a little bit cheesy, but hopefully they'll help illustrate some of these green-focused concepts in a more relatable way.

When I say that this work is personal to me, I mean it. My family has been in the horticulture and nursery business since the early 1900s. My great-great-great grandpa started our family's nursery business in 1905 and it's still going today. I am a fifth-generation family member working at the company, which is now one of the largest growers of shrubs and trees in the United States. Three generations of family members work in the business today, including my grandpa, mom, and brother. It's an incredibly unique phenomenon, and one that I wouldn't trade for the world.

Whether your style is casual and wild or formal and modern, you'll find the right garden fit for you.

(BELOW) A welcoming space that is a reflection of you is the end goal, regardless of whether your vibe is cozy, chic, or tailored.

Our company's slogan used to be "our roots run deep," and while we don't use that any longer, it really resonates with me. Generations of our blood-related family and our family of employees have grown hundreds of millions of plants that now cover the whole world. My great uncle, Gordie Bailey, recently told a story about how, while driving to work now, he sees plants that he and his father put in the ground many decades ago that are still blooming and creating a beautiful backdrop to life for all that pass through those streets. How crazy and impactful is that? Putting a shrub in the ground may seem somewhat insignificant in the grand scheme of things, but to drive down a road or look out your window or see a photo of a place where, decades before, you dug your hands in the dirt and created a home for a plant that is still thriving today. Well, I think that's incredible.

And that's what we're doing here. Of course, we're making a beautiful place for you, your friends, and family to enjoy now. But you also have the opportunity to create a lifelong tapestry of life in your landscape. There's an old Chinese proverb that says "The best time to plant a tree was 20 years ago. The second best time is now." So, let's get going! As we dive into this book, we're going to have fun. I'm going to assign homework (don't worry, it'll be fun and involve food and drinks). You're going to learn a little bit more about yourself and your goals at home. And your yard is going to transform into the oasis that is exactly perfect for you.

This will not be your standard garden design book. It's truly a celebration of you. We're going to take some moments out of your crazy schedule to discover what you enjoy. We're going to celebrate color, texture, seasonality, and so much more. Life is beyond hectic, so sometimes you just need some *you time*. Well, now it's going to be *me and you time*, but it'll be a blast. We're going to start outside the gardening world and then weave our way back before getting to planting plans. So, if you're reading Chapter 1 and wondering if you picked up the wrong book, you didn't. We're just doing a little exploration so that when we get to recipe cards for your yard, you're picking what is best for your personal aesthetic, understanding what nature's going to provide for free, and knowing what you want to put in and what you want to get out of the landscape. It's a windy road, but we're going to get there. I promise.

Before we dive in, I want to thank you again. I take to heart the trust and faith you're putting into this process. I hope to make you smile, make you think, and get you excited to get those hands dirty. While we're going to go through some functional processes, this should be fun. It's art, remember? I'm going to spend the next 200 pages telling you how to play in your yard. We're going on dates, talking about fashion, and creating recipes. Not to mention cocktails. It's like those painting classes with friends where you can bring a bottle of wine, but at the end of it, you've got something beautiful and lasting that will hang in your home for years.

Whether you consider yourself a budding gardener, a Master Gardener, or #notagardener (check out the Instagram hashtag), this book is all in your honor. No matter your experience or background in horticulture or anything green, you'll glean some helpful nuggets of inspiration from these pages. And in the end, my hope is that you walk away with a personalized, special, and long-lasting design for your home. Because at the end of the day, this outdoor space is one of the ways to make your house a home. That's the beauty and power of plants. They transform a blank canvas into something special. And it's even more special when you're the painter behind the work.

So, let's get started. Roll up your sleeves and get ready. It's time to dig in and make your landscape dreams come true.

1

Polka Dots or Stripes

"Style is something each of us already has, all we need to do is find it."

—DIANE VON FURSTENBERG

STYLE IS SUBJECTIVE. What I think is cute might make you shudder. What sparks joy for you might not be my cup of tea. But that's fine. Variety is the spice of life, right? While there are boxes constructed around style to help understand aesthetic patterns, our unique perspectives are what creates such a beautiful world. The little black dress. A midcentury modern couch. The Sydney Opera House. Icons of style across disciplines make an instant statement tied to emotion.

Our choices around style, fashion, architecture, and furniture all say a lot about our outlook on life. But this isn't a psychology book. This is, at the end of the day, a garden design book. So, we're not going to go too deep into the psychology around choice in style, but rather use it as a framework for how we create a sense of home. It's about helping us choose a collection of plants (often called a plant palette) that is aesthetically pleasing so that we can enjoy it for years to come. Because designing and planting a garden is not just for today. In fact, it's not for today at all but really for tomorrow, for next week, for next year, and for years down the road.

Falling off the pages of any architectural magazine, this dreamscape of a pool house is my cotton candy sunset heaven. I love the clean lines of the building and opening that gives a peek into the pool. It sparks joy for me. How about you?

You don't have to love fashion. You don't have to be an interior designer. You don't have to study architecture. Just know that what pleases you acts as a starting point. At the end of this journey, I will make sure that you have a beautiful idea of where you're going to go with your outside design. Also, remember that there's a difference between what you like for you and what you like on someone else. The same can be said about what you see in someone else's yard and what you like for your own. Are you appreciating this style because you think it looks great on Audrey Hepburn, but you would never wear it yourself? Do you love that design in *Elle Décor*, but would you actually use it in your own house? That's what we are trying to determine in this chapter. Let's take your style and what you appreciate, and make it fit your lifestyle, what work you want to do, and what fits in your budget.

Throughout this book, I'm going to ask you to do some observational homework. Don't worry, it's not real homework. It's watching-TV-and-having-drinks kind of homework, so it'll be fun. Before we get to deeper plant talk, we're going to explore your interests, the function of your home environment, and set some expectations for the work you want to put in and what you want to get out of your landscape. We'll start with your aesthetic. Pay attention to some of the topics I mention throughout Chapter 1 and you just might see them pop back up again in Chapter 4 as we break down design elements for your outdoor space. Wink wink.

Fashion

I'll start by saying that I am no fashionista. Troll my Instagram and you'll see that I can throw a look together, but it's not going to make the pages of *Vogue*. But that's not to say that I can't appreciate some amazing fashion for all that it's worth. This informs my decision-making as it relates to my home, my garden, and my day-to-day purchases. I drool over a Thom Browne suit and kilt, but can I pull it off? I'm not Dan Levy, so probably not as well as I do in my mind's eye. But I love what it says about the *Schitt's Creek* genius and his personality when he rocks those amazing looks. Just because it isn't right for me doesn't mean that it doesn't inform my aesthetic. The bold personality, powerful message, and contrast of expectation and reality resonate with me. So, how does fashion inspire your life? Let's look at a few ways you may be influenced, consciously or otherwise.

Finding your garden style starts with examining your own sense of aesthetics and your taste in fashion, furniture, and more.

Bright pops of color from plants or furniture can create certain feelings and create a strong statement. Is it for you? Maybe yes, maybe no.

This front entrance garden is filled with different textures from the plants and the hardscaping. Your taste in textures should be reflected in your garden.

COLOR. When I think of fashion, I think of bold choices in color. Whether that's choosing to be bold with monochrome or blasting an array of color, all aspects of fashion can make a bold statement. How people choose to implement color—or lack thereof—is intentional. A James Bond–style Tom Ford suit exudes sex, power, and confidence. A patterned, colorful Diane von Furstenberg wrap dress says fun, outgoing, and empowered. Color can shape personality, or at least the perception of personality. Making decisions around how you use color in your home will create that feeling immediately. A more traditional design won't likely showcase a mix of bright colors but would rather incorporate swaths of unified colors. A more modern design may be a bit bolder, embracing a monochromatic palette or one with bright colors to make a strong statement. As you start to become aware of the color scheme that resonates with you, don't be shy to move outside your comfort zone and think about what makes you happy in your surroundings. Even if you're a shy person, you can still embrace color and vice versa.

TEXTURE. When you try clothes on, the feeling of certain fabrics can make or break the decision to purchase. Beyond color, this is one of my favorite things about fashion. Not only does texture make a piece of clothing more or less wearable, but it makes such a difference in the perception of the garment and how it pairs with other pieces of clothing. A unique fabric or pattern can really elevate an ensemble and take it from fine to fab. Do you like cotton, linen, tweed, polyester, or denim? How do each make you feel and how do you think you're perceived in each?

As summer turns to fall in this garden, the changing foliage alters the appearance of the landscape. Design your garden to be interesting in all seasons.

Shapes and edges tell stories in a garden. The way the edges of the concrete and the planting beds mimic the silhouette of the rock in the foreground creates a unified sense of place.

Again, I'm not trying to dive deep into your psyche but just trying to get you to think about how texture plays out in your everyday life, and then I promise I'll bring it back to the garden.

SEASONALITY. Spring raincoats, summer shorts, fall sweaters, and winter boots. When you live in a region with four seasons, you hopefully understand these all-important items for seasonal living. Coming from Minnesota, we are deeply involved in each of these seasons, so we have different closets for each season. Each season is unique and deserves its own wardrobe. Not just for fashion, but ultimately for function. If you don't live in an area with sub-zero temperatures, the idea of a winter closet may be a foreign concept, but it is real life and without it we'd be stuck inside for months. As someone who experiences all four seasons every year, it's such an amazing treat. We get to celebrate nature in all its glory 365 days a year and translating that into the garden is the gift that keeps on giving. Whether you have one season or four, planning your landscape for the time of year is like planning your closet; it needs some rotation to accommodate Mother Nature.

SHAPE. I was just having a conversation about flare jeans. I loved rocking them in high school (as my parents did during their high school years), but we've been stuck in skinny jeans in recent memory. I personally vote for a return to the flare, but that's for another book.

What this is all about is creating silhouettes. Shape tells its own story. Sleek lines, billowy ambiguity, and a combination thereof all say different things. Think of classic beauties such as Farrah Fawcett and Audrey Hepburn. Stunning in their own right, but incredibly different in their fashion choices. Farrah with form-fitting tops and bellbottoms, and Audrey with cigarette pants and a turtleneck. The silhouette they created transcends their own celebrity and echoes the era in which they lived. Those silhouettes elicit emotion, establish time, and give an understanding to the greater context of the culture in which they lived. Again, not a commentary on these fabulous women, but rather an illustration about how their iconic fashion has meaning. You can do this with your landscape design too. Stay tuned!

PATTERN. I'm a sucker for clean lines, but adding something extra to a shirt can be the difference between me walking by a rack and pulling off an item to try on. My sister is a major polka dot person. If she sees anything with polka dots, all bets are off. Me, on the other hand, I'm a stripes kind of guy. Vertical, not horizontal—because I'm not a monster. Or thin enough to pull off a horizontal stripe. But that's beside the point. Patterns bring a sense of consistency and structure to a garment. My sister and I can agree on that at least. Putting like objects in a row gives a sense of calm and continuity. On the flip side, contrasting patterns, textures, or colors also have major impact. This dichotomy of unity and contrast has a residency in modern fashion, but also in our landscapes whether we know it or not. Whether you choose to celebrate communion or tension is your decision, but I'll help you to that final call as it relates to your garden in the coming chapters. Beyond the garden, that's on you, friend!

Furniture

Recently, my husband and I bought our first house together. I'll talk about the landscape design process throughout this book, but first let me start by telling you how many times we went furniture shopping. It might have been excessive. But furniture is more than just comfort. It dictates how you use a space and the feeling of a room; it adds structure. Bringing pieces in changes everything about a home, and so taking the time to realize their impact—and what is most important to you—can inform decision-making for the outdoor space.

FUNCTION. Of course, furniture dictates function. Chairs are necessary for sitting just like a table is necessary for eating. What I'm getting at here goes a bit deeper. Think about why you chose your couch, for example. Why did you choose that size? Did you want to close off one side of the room with a chaise or did you want to create separation in an open concept? Look at the overall structure and the lines that each piece creates. How do the shape and size affect the layout and feeling of the room? These big pieces can establish flow based on how you want people to experience the space. As you're making any design plan, inside or out, remember that you have the control for how your family and guests interact with your home. Pretty darn cool. As you're out and about, pay attention to how others have set up the furniture in their homes. Do they have oversized furniture or sleek, trim furnishings? Then ask yourself why.

(OPPOSITE, TOP) Furniture adds structure and functionality to a space. The faux wicker and comfy cushions of this patio set compliment the casual, cottage feel of the garden.

(OPPOSITE, BOTTOM) What is the function of each piece of furniture you place in your garden, and how does it affect the flow of foot traffic or how people use and experience the space? The bright colors of these Adirondack chairs evoke a different feeling than muted shades.

The natural tones of the wood deck, chairs, and table echo the wood tones of the fence and plant materials. This adds a sense of warmth and softens the sharp lines to make a modern space feel comfortable.

PERSONALITY. Let's spice things up a bit, huh? Furniture really says a lot about you. One of the most fun things about designing a house is all the amazing colors, textures, shapes, and sizes you can use to fill a room. Area rugs, throw pillows, artwork, plates, shelves, bar carts, and on and on. I consider myself a fairly traditional guy when it comes to design. My office has a gray rug, white planters for my houseplants, and minimalist furniture. But I'm not so traditional that I can't add some big pops of color. In fact, I've got a 5- x 6-foot (150- x 180-cm) floral painting of all color behind my desk. It's my personality to a T. Clean, sleek lines with muted colors and then bam . . . some fun and festive color to brighten up your day. People know when they walk into my office the kind of person they're going to meet. Traditional, mid-century, contemporary, rustic, boho, French country—there are so many terms for furniture styles. Where do you fit and what does it say about your aesthetic?

HARMONY. Furniture and accessories also have the ability to create unity or contrast, and in both of those instances, they add to the personality of the space. We've all heard of feng shui, right? The ancient Chinese practice is all about using furniture to create harmony and balance. The materials, colors, and shapes of furniture influence the energy and feeling of a room. Feng shui promotes a balance of five natural elements—earth, fire, wood, water, and metal—throughout your home, with each element assigned to the purpose of each room. Now, just like this isn't a psychology book, it's also not an interior design book, but using the overriding principle of balance and harmony by using physical objects is relative to the garden too. As we work from the living room to the outdoors in Chapter 4, I'll help you create balance in your landscape for clarity, definition, and legibility. Even if you prefer a looser, more natural look, balance will keep your landscape from chaos.

The furniture you choose should be in perfect harmony with its overall surroundings. The material, structure, and color of this high top coordinate beautifully with the desert plantings and tile-roofed home.

Whether your home boasts modern architecture, like this one, or is a sweet old Victorian, you can create a garden that complements it beautifully.

Architecture

Whether you're a Frank Lloyd Wright aficionado or never understood the difference between Georgian and Renaissance design, it doesn't matter. Architecture surrounds us every day, and there's a lot we can learn from our reaction to it. From Gaudi's Gothic Revival masterpiece, the Basílica de la Sagrada Família, to Frank Geary's Walt Disney Concert Hall, the marvels of architecture create sometimes polarizing and often awe-inducing emotions. What we can take from reviewing architecture—even these massive projects—can help us understand how to make our own homes special and unique.

SCALE. Scale is one of the first things you notice about a building. Not just the size of the building, but how it relates to the world around it, which is what is meant when we talk about proportions. Many of the foundational principles are based on the golden ratio. Without going into a bunch of mathematical formulas, the golden ratio appears in nature over and over, creating a visually appealing and balanced object. Think of the swirl of rose petals, a whirlpool, conch shells, or a spider web. There's a visual pattern of consistency that all ties back to this golden ratio number of 1.618. Architects use this formula to determine the base scale of wall height, the space between windows, the overall height versus width of buildings, doorways, and so much more. Everything from the Parthenon and Notre Dame to the CN Tower in Toronto have been built using this mathematical formula to achieve balance. Foundational elements of architecture still are

The scale of these planting beds is in proportion with the width of the walkway and angles of the house. This creates balance.

Sight lines draw the eye through a landscape. They also draw people out the door and into the garden.

driven by this so-called perfect number, and then adjust proportions for impact. Oversized windows draw in more natural light, making a room feel larger than it is, for example. Scale gives us the size of an object or a project whereas proportion speaks to the size of one object, or piece of an object, as it relates to the larger whole. So, while you're out walking the dog, see which of your neighbors' houses feel in balance and in proportion to their lot size, and then look to see if their architects made any adjustments to the scale or proportion of the build and why.

VIEWS. With any construction project, you always have to think about sight lines. What do you want people to see and what do you want hidden? How do certain choices in building materials draw the visitor's eyes through the space? Remember, as we just talked about, you have control over how people engage with your home. Architects have the same experience with sight lines.

The ever-popular open floor plan makes a home feel larger, allowing your eyes to move from one room to another and then, typically, to the outdoors. Without having a visual barrier, our brains are tricked into thinking a 10×10-foot room feels twice that size. On the flipside, architects will use tricks to hide pieces of the home that you may not want to see, like a toilet or the entrance to the master bedroom. By adding walls or moving less glamourous parts of the house out of the sight line through a doorway, it makes those spaces more intimate and, by not drawing the eye toward it, will keep people out of your personal business. Let's face it, we don't want anyone rummaging through our medicine cabinet, so if something as simple as sight lines can deter people from our private quarters, I'm all for it.

MOMENTS. What's life without special moments? Those special times when the light hits just right and you let out a joyful sigh. When everything just feels right in the world. While the chaos of our lives may not lend itself to experiencing those fleeting moments often enough, designers work to incorporate physical spaces for those aha moments. Adding a transom window on a west-facing wall to let that golden-hour light peek in, or an east-facing private master deck for morning coffee while the sun rises can elevate a space from mundane to magic. Even reading about those spaces makes me feel good. I hope it does for you too. What are the special places in your home where you can have those little moments of solace? What about growing up? Maybe it was your parents' or grandparents' home that brings back warm, fuzzy memories. What made that so special? As we move forward and bring these concepts into the outdoor world, think about how the structure and light of your home create those special moments.

Starting this journey of planning your outside space with some contextual examples of fashion, furniture, and architecture hopefully will give you a foundational understanding of basic concepts that we'll pull out in Chapter 4. Having some real-life examples will break down some of the scary walls that you might have up as we move into this world of living plants and spending money on irrigation. Because this shouldn't be scary. We're going to have some fun with it!

Finding what makes your outdoor space special to you and your loved ones makes the journey worth it.

2

Date Night with Your Space

"Design is not just what it looks like and feels like. Design is how it works."

—STEVE JOBS

BEFORE YOU PUT pen to paper or start plant shopping, you've got to take a step back and assess the situation at home. Making a design without knowing the fundamentals about your space is like starting to bake a cake without checking to see if you have flour or eggs on hand. So, it's time for a little bit of a yard check to see what you're working with. This chapter is about setting some time aside for date nights at home. You can include your spouse, partner, friends, family, and kids. This is going to be fun, remember? Let's get them all involved! This journey to learning and loving your yard—possibly in a new way—is going to set you up for the best success as you beautify that space.

First, let's set some ground rules, starting with the most important one: Enjoy yourself along the way. Keep in mind that this is an ongoing journey that is all about creating a beautiful, functional, and ever-changing space to meet your and your family's needs. This is just the first step in understanding what your landscape has to offer and how you can maximize those assets to meet your goals. Don't get bogged down in too much structure or detail in this early part of the process. Plants and garden design can seem daunting and scary, but I'm here to help alleviate that so you truly can enjoy the process as much as the results.

Sit back, relax, and have some fun with this process. Make yourself a charcuterie board and get to planning.

Second ground rule: Don't fight nature. Throughout this chapter, I will encourage you to pay attention to what's organically happening around you to give direction for what to plant. Mother Nature is the be-all and end-all. She is in charge, not us. Paying attention to when and where the sun hits your yard, what kind of soil you have, the temperature extremes of your region, and more plays into where and how we start building your plant lists. There might be a gorgeous garden you see on Instagram, but if it's in a really different hardiness zone (if this means nothing to you at this point don't worry, we'll talk about this soon), none of those plants will survive in your climate. So having a foundation of what will and will not work will come from this intentional focus on your natural surroundings.

Third ground rule: Pay attention to your surrounding community. Of course, your landscape is going to be unique to you and your style. That's why you're reading this book in the first place. But getting inspiration from your neighbors will help you make decisions about your own yard. It might be things you love, and

While this desert home landscape may not work in your climate, you can still take inspiration from it. As you travel around your own community, look for local inspiration. Keep your eyes open to all the possibilities, no matter what kind of growing conditions you have.

it might be things you see and realize you definitely don't want to see in your own landscape. As I mentioned, I purchased a new home and within months had to replace the roof after a hailstorm. Bummer, right? As we were selecting the shingle color, I suddenly started realizing what color shingles were on the homes in our neighborhood. As I walked my dog along the trails and through the streets, something as blatant as the roof color that I had ignored for months was jumping out at me at every turn. Now I had a reason to look, and I couldn't unsee it. So, as you start the design process for your outdoor space, keep your eyes peeled for what you love and what you can do without.

Now that we've got the ground rules set, let's start making plans. The rest of this chapter will give you "home date" ideas for different parts of your day. Each date will check a box for something you need to remember when we actually get to planning your garden and choosing plant recipes in Chapter 5. Let's plan some date days!

Coffee Talk

DATE IDEA	***Morning walk***
DRINK	***Coffee (iced or hot, depending on the season), hot chocolate, or berries plus bubbly (soda water or champagne . . . who am I to judge?!)***
THE "WHY"	***Getting an idea of the aesthetic in your surroundings***

Now I'm not here to tell you to copy your neighbors. In fact, I'm here to tell you that you can do better. But getting an idea of what's going on in your neighborhood, subdivision, or nearby community can give you a starting point: inspiration for design elements you like (or really don't like), plants that survive and thrive in your microclimate, color combinations that catch your eye, and guidelines for what's allowed if you're in an association-managed community.

Starting your day with a morning walk not only helps with mental clarity, but it is a great time for a close-up with your neighbors' yards that you may not notice as you breeze by in your car. So, grab your coffee (or some bubbly and berries with a friend) and get out for a walk to start your day on the right foot, pun intended. And while you're at it, let's check off some landscape design to-dos. See, I promised this could be fun and fit into your daily routine! Here's what you should be looking for as you meander the neighborhood. Keep in mind you don't need to do all of this at once. You want to enjoy your walk too, so parcel out these attributes over a couple of weeks on your morning walks. Take your time. Remember that planting a garden is a long-term investment, so there's no need to rush the planning process.

There's lots to see here with Endless Summer® The Original Hydrangea shielding both sides of a Japanese maple, hostas, ornamental grasses, and more. And that morning light really makes it shine. This is a really inviting sidewalk presentation that captures attention as you walk, bike, or drive by.

Color

As we talked about in Chapter 1, how you enjoy or appreciate color will ultimately impact your plant selection. Now's the time to give things a test run without having to purchase, plant, and maintain something in your own garden. As you're taking a walk, use the Notes app on your phone or take photos (with permission; don't make it creepy) of what catches your eye. Don't forget to note *why* it caught your eye; you'll end up with a library of notes. Keeping track of the why will help when you get to choosing your plant palate. Look for patterns of color that stand out.

Is it the blues and purples or yellows and oranges that bring you joy? Or are you noticing the different color of leaves more often? Don't forget to look at how colors play together too. Look at the color of houses, their fence or hardscaping, and then how the plants complement or contrast those physical structures. Which do you prefer—a complementary color scheme or one with a bolder impact? As you get closer to home, look at what color scheme exists already. Without looking, could you say exactly what color your roof or hardscaping elements are? It's human nature to become blind to the things we see every day, so if you couldn't give a good description of your own house, that's totally natural! That's why we're doing this; we're taking some time to date our house and get even more familiar with our space before we build this investment of a landscape.

This display of annuals and perennials makes a bold statement, mixing warm and cool colors balanced by neutral white plants. Note if this caught your eye because you loved it or if it wasn't your speed.

Size

The scale and scope of gardens and plants is really important to understand. Are you working with an urban, postage stamp-size lot; a suburban plot with some space to breathe; or do you have lots of space to fill? As you take your morning walk, pay attention to how large the lots and landscaped spaces are in comparison to your own. An understanding of scale will be important as you begin to focus on how much work it will take to plant and maintain your garden, as well as how much budget you'll need to set aside (we'll talk about more about budget in Chapter 3). That being said, don't be scared off by large-scale plantings. I'll be sure to give you options that use fewer plants for big impact. To that end, pay attention to the size of the plants in the landscape. Which plant immediately caught your eye because it serves as a focal point? Was it a tree or larger shrub protruding from the underplanted garden? Be on the lookout for the way plant sizes add layers to the garden and make note of which patterns really draw your attention.

The size of your space will determine the scale of your plantings and hardscape. The statue in this large garden serves as a welcome focal point to draw your attention and provide a sense of scale.

Plant Combos

One of the most fun things to do as you plan your landscape is to find plants that go well together. It's one of those daunting tasks as you start out, especially if you look up pre-made landscape designs online. Getting your head around mature size, spacing, color combinations, and all the other considerations is enough to make your head spin right off. So, let's keep the focus on making it easy for you! On one of your morning walks, pay attention to which groupings of plants really appeal to you. Look at how the colors work together, how different size plants play off each other, and if plant textures catch your eye. Remember what I suggested about noting color: patterns of yellow and purple, cream and green, blue and orange, etc. Watch how groundcovers may have an obelisk-shaped plant peeking out above them or how fine-textured ornamental grasses are placed near broad-leaf plants such as hostas or hydrangeas. These contrasting shapes and textures are intentional; they make your space less boring and capture attention. Observing how flowers and leaves are placed next to each other can help you figure out your preference. Don't forget: You're not making any design decisions yet. You're just looking at what you like and don't like so we can narrow plant selection down in Chapters 4 and 5. Keep those notes going so you can remember what you like later.

The yellow of the black-eyed Susans and the purple of the chairs in this small front yard planting add brightness to the space. Plus, the mixture of various textures provides additional interest.

Deco Pots + Hardscaping

As much as I'm a plantsperson, I also love the balancing act of incorporating decorative pots, hardscaping, garden art, and water features when it's appropriate. Now, my personal style is a bit more minimalist, but I'm not here to push my aesthetic on you. I'm here to give you all sorts of ideas that you can incorporate to make your garden your own. So, if you want to fill your garden with art and water, go for it!

I'll help you pick planting schemes that will accent and support your design. But first, let's get back to our morning date. As you're meandering the neighborhood with your drink of choice, one of your other goals is to see what the neighbors have for these hard surfaces. You might see deco pots on a front step, a retaining wall or pavers leading to the backyard, hear the sound of a waterfall babbling down a hillside, or see a metal frog in the front garden. Again, no judgement here. If you want a frog, get yourself a frog! What you want to pay attention to in this phase of planning are a few key elements:

1. Where are those deco pots placed, what's planted in them, and what color are the pots?
2. Where did they use hardscaping such as a retaining wall or pavers, what colors are used, and how are the plants used in combination with the hard surfaces?
3. How and where are garden sculptures or water used in the space?

Jot down the things you liked or didn't like so you've got a record of it when it's time to build out your own garden. I promise you'll never remember everything when the rubber hits the road at home, even if your memory is better than my guppy brain.

The stone patio, rustic table, and water feature in this garden match the aesthetic of the natural planting scheme perfectly.

Brunch

DATE IDEA	***Midmorning meal + science***
DRINK	***Champagne-based cocktails, coffee and juice bar, or bubbly waters***
THE "WHY"	***Learning the soil composition of your garden beds***

I know this date is a little bit of bribery for your friends, but who doesn't love a little brunch mixed with a science experiment? Who knows, maybe they'll learn something and be inspired to go home and learn about their garden too! Okay, so here's the deal. For this date, we're going to learn a bit about the natural soil composition in your yard. Not super sexy, I know, but it's one of the most important things to learn for the ultimate success of your landscape. Back to the home foundation analogy: If you don't start on solid ground, you're destined for failure. Getting

(OPPOSITE) This home maximized a small space by incorporating a Zen garden into the backyard with a modern koi pond, straight line hardscaping, and decorative pots with colorful and textural annuals.

(ABOVE) It's not glamorous, but knowing what kind of soil you have in your garden can improve your chances of creating a successful outdoor growing space. Don't let these gorgeous blooms fool you. They wouldn't be there if it weren't for healthy soil.

to know what makes up your dirt will help you know what work needs to be done to amend it, if necessary, or how to choose plants that work with the natural mix of the dirt in your yard.

Here's where the experiment starts. When you invite everyone over, have them bring a jar of dirt from their garden (or where they'd like to start planting) and dig up a shovel full of dirt from your future garden space. It's no quiche, but it'll do for this brunch. *By the way, at this party you might need to provide all the snacks and drinks since everyone else is bringing dirt . . . sorry!* While you're snacking and having a beverage, you're each going to do what is known as the Jar Test. This is going to help you determine the general mix of silt, sand, and clay in your soil so you can make the best plant decisions. Remember, this is going to give you a high-level look at the mix, and if you want to learn more about the nutrients and elements in your soil, you can purchase a soil testing kit from your local garden center or connect with a local agricultural service office for a more in-depth soil test. But for our day date purposes, the Jar Test is going to give you enough information to get started.

Once you do the experiment, you'll know what combination of soil is in your yard and then it's time to figure out what the heck that means. Some of you may have one clear winner while others might have a combination of soil types. Either way, you'll be able to glean some tidbits of best practices with these tips and tricks. Now remember that this is just a starting point. If you determine that you don't love the soil you've got and want to amend it to better suit the plants you're looking for, we'll chat more about that in Chapter 4.

(NEXT SPREAD) The type of soil you have in your garden can impact what plants will grow successfully there, but it's good to know that you can improve the soil if you don't have ideal conditions.

THE JAR TEST

Without getting too deep in the mud now (pun intended), let's look at some basic information on soil. In Chapter 4, we'll look a bit more on amending soil, if that's the route you decide to go. This will give you an idea of what is naturally happening in your landscape, so if you don't want to do a ton of work, you can plan accordingly based on your soil. Remember to download and use your Date Night Checklists so you can track your soil type or types; it's going to play a big part of what plant pairings and recipe cards are best used in your yard once we get to Chapter 5.

Doing the Jar Test itself is pretty darn easy, and it's quick in the moment so you can get back to brunching with your friends. Fill a clear mason jar with about two-thirds water and then add enough of the soil from your yard to just about fill it. That's it—for now! Back to mimosas. While you're sipping and noshing away, share some of the advice from the next pages with your friends so when they figure out what kind of soil they have, they know what to do.

Okay, so after brunch and everyone goes home, let them know not touch the jars for a couple of days so everything can settle. The sand will settle to the bottom, silt in the middle, and clay on top. It'll take some time for this all to settle out, so set it and forget it for a bit. Once you see clearly delineated rows, bust out your ruler and calculator. I know, back to high school, but I'll make this easy for you.

- Measure the distance from the base of the jar to the top of the three layers.
- Then measure the height of each individual layer.
- Divide the layer height by the overall height to calculate the percentage of each element in your home soil mix.
- Use this handy graphic below from the United States Department of Agriculture (USDA) to figure out what you're working with so you can make the right plant choices.

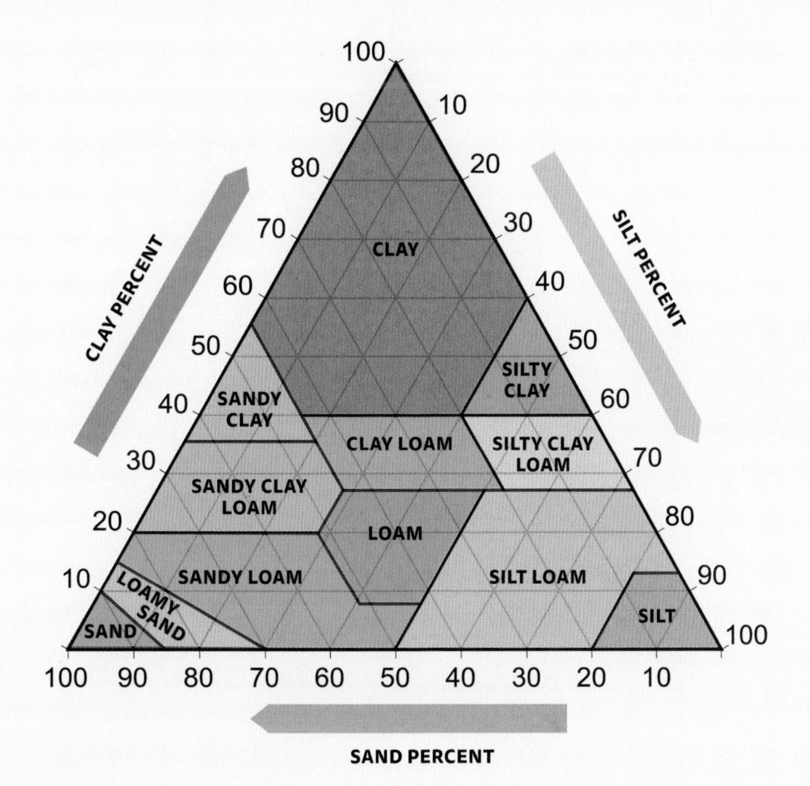

Sandy Soil

If your Jar Test told you that you've got sandy soil, this means that water and nutrients may run away from the root system of your plants fairly quickly, but that doesn't mean that sandy soil is bad for all plants. Remember, different plants do well in different types of soil, especially when you talk about plants that are native to regions with more sandy soil. Plants such as lavender, sedum, and chaste tree thrive in sandy soil because they come from global regions with harsher soil conditions that are higher in sand. Vegetables such as potatoes, onion, and carrots also do well in sandy soil because it's a bit looser and allows their root systems to expand and makes the harvesting process easier.

The sandy soil beneath this garden means it is well-drained and welcoming to plants such as lavender, red hot pokers, and spurges.

Silt Soil

This type of soil isn't very common unless you're really near a riverbed, but if you've got silt in your soil mix, count yourself lucky. Silt particles are in between the size of sand and clay, so it's sort of the best of both worlds in that it can retain moisture and nutrients without being so compacted that it doesn't allow drainage. Now, a mostly silt mix isn't the best of the best, but it's pretty darn good. Think of that sludgy feel when you walk into a river bottom. It's still a little dense and holds more moisture than is ideal for most plants, but it's better than the other extremes. Plants such as dogwood, buttonbush, willow, and iris can thrive in this type of environment since they can tolerate "wet feet" (which is gardener talk for roots that can handle sitting in a bit of water longer than most).

Clay Soil

One of the trickiest soil types, especially if you're just getting started or don't want to do a ton of work, is clay. Clay is heavy and dense, making it tough for the roots of certain plants to establish. It can get water-logged in winter and spring since it retains a lot of moisture and then can bake into a solid mass in the heat of summer. Both situations make it tough for oxygen and water to move around the soil and benefit the roots. Of all soil types, this is one that I mostly recommend amending. That said, not all hope is lost if you've got clay soil and don't want to go through the work of adding anything. Plants such as big bluestem ornamental grass, asters, coneflowers, sedum, and daylilies can all tolerate clay. So, color and texture are still possible even without amending. I promised there's still hope, didn't I?

This lovely patio planting consists of plants that thrive in dense, clay-based soils.

Loam Soil

As you did the Jar Test, I asked you to measure sand, silt, and clay. Not loam. But that's because loam is a soil texture that consists of a pretty even split of all three components, with maybe a tinge less clay than sand and silt. This is the gold standard for gardeners. Loamy soil retains water but doesn't get waterlogged, and it drains, but not so much that all the nutrients and water run away from the plants' roots. This one really is the best of all worlds (sorry, silt). If you're lucky enough to have a variation on loam soil, you better brag to your friends at the next brunch get-together because all you have to do is stick your shovel in the ground, plop the plant in, and water. Okay, there's more to it than that, but you won't have to do much—if any—soil amending to achieve optimal planting conditions.

This was an extended date day because it's so important. Like I said before we got into all this testing: It's the foundation of your garden, so you've got to know what you're working with or you won't have success. It's about setting expectations and boundaries and making the right plans. This date is just setting the stage for what's to come, so don't get too stressed yet if your soil type doesn't seem like it's going to give you a beautiful garden. It's all workable, and we'll sort through what that means in Chapters 4 and 5, where we start coming up with solutions. The fun continues!

Getting to know your soil before starting the garden design and plant selection process leads to a greater chance of a successful (and beautiful!) outdoor living space.

Luncheon

DATE IDEA	***Picnic in the yard***
DRINK	***Arnold Palmer, fresh-squeezed lemonade, or spritz cocktail***
THE "WHY"	***Understanding your planting zone***

I don't care how crazy this sounds, but it's time to act like you're going to Central Park and pack up a picnic lunch. Get the kids involved if you have them, convince your partner that it's going to be fun, or take yourself on a hot solo date to soak up the sun. There are no rules when it comes to dating your space, as long as you answer the "Why" when it's all said and done.

During this lunch hour, you're going to learn all about the regionality of planting and how where you live affects what goes in the ground. Stepping back, it all makes sense and seems obvious. You don't naturally see palm trees in Minnesota, and on the flip side, you don't see peonies in southern Florida. But until you are faced with it, there's really no reason to think

The palm trees in the background of this image tell you that this garden is in a warm growing zone. Get familiar with your climate, including the temperatures, elevation, and precipitation, before tackling your design project.

about weather patterns affecting your plants beyond a late spring frost zapping your annuals or vegetable garden. We'll talk a bit about how to figure out what your planting zone is, what that means, and why it's not a hard and fast guideline. We'll also dive into other regional aspects of planting, including elevation, precipitation levels, and native plants and related cultivated native selections. I know it seems like a lot for your lunch break, but we'll answer the most important questions to get started and then you can dig a bit deeper post-date in Chapter 4.

Plant Climate Zones

If you have to pick the most important starting point for determining how your location affects what you can and cannot plant, it's understanding your plant climate zone. This means average winter temperatures and heat summer extremes, which give you a frame of reference for what plants can survive the harshest temperatures your region is likely to experience. In my area of Minnesota, for example, I can expect the coldest winter temperatures to be between -25° to -20°F (-32° to -29°C). Yes, it gets really cold here in Minnesota, and yes, we can still grow gorgeous gardens! This understanding allows me to know that I can successfully grow a lilac (*Syringa* spp.) but not a crape myrtle (*Lagerstroemia* spp.), narrowing the scope of my plant palette and making selection less scary.

On the flip side of cold hardiness is understanding how plants can handle the heat. This is especially important for warmer climates because, while you do have to worry about the cold temperatures nipping your more tender plants in the winter months, you do have to be careful that the heat doesn't take too much out of them either. Look at how many days you experience extreme heat—a good starting point is the average number of days above 86°F or 30°C. This also can help narrow your plant selection. When looking at a plant for your yard, research how they can not only handle heat, but how they thrive in consistently warm temperatures. Throwing it back to the cold climate example, many lilacs can survive in warmer temperatures, but they don't bloom because they need more cold days than warm days. And plants like gardenia (*Gardenia* spp.) thrive on moderate heat and won't survive cold. So, first get an understanding of your climate and then choose plants that will thrive in it. A good, local nursery can prove very helpful in your research because they will only sell plants that are suitable to the region where they are located. As a side note, for those of you in moderate climates, be sure to pay attention to the extremes of both cold and heat.

(OPPOSITE) This cold-climate front yard planting relies on very hardy plants, such as the weeping Alaska cedar, juniper, and other hardy evergreens, to provide color and texture.

Elevation

One deviation from the climate and hardiness standard is high elevation gardening. When you live in a place with variations in terrain, it also can affect what plants do well for you. Indirect sunlight, rocky ground, shortened growing season, and fluctuations in temperature are more prevalent at higher altitudes. So even if your climate tells you that your temperatures are appropriate for certain plants, your selection may be actually altered because you have less sunlight or more dramatic temperature fluctuations than someone

else who has the same minimum winter temperatures as you do but is at a lower elevation.

If you're in this situation, there are a couple of things to consider. First, connect with a local gardening expert or a local university or governmental agricultural program that may be able to give you some insight into the nuances of your region. The other advice is to allow some trial and error to occur. I know that's not the best (or most cost-efficient) answer, but nature isn't black and white. There are pockets of uniqueness called microclimates, meaning that your region's climate might have average winter temperatures as low as 15°F (-9C), but your home may be able to sustain plants that have a minimum temperature tolerance below that because of pockets of warmth, additional water supply, or added protection from wind or fluctuating temperatures. If you're struggling a bit, stick with more cold-tolerant plants and try different species of plants that have different sun and soil needs. Consider that your ground may have a unique nutrient makeup that is more alkaline or acidic, which can affect a plant's performance. Remember that this is something you also can get tested to get specific answers for your home garden. And don't forget: We all kill plants. That's a part of this journey. And when one plant doesn't survive, you'll learn something from it and have the opportunity to try something new! There's always a silver lining.

Gardening at higher elevation can create the opportunity for stunning landscapes like this mountain retreat in Colorado filled with clustered bellflower (*Campanula glomerata*)) and yarrow (*Achillea millefolium*).

Precipitation

It probably doesn't come as a big surprise that water affects what plants grow and thrive. But as it relates to looking beyond your climate, it's really important to take note of your average rainfall. For example, both Miami, Florida, and Los Angeles, California, have similar climates as it relates to temperature, but Miami averages over 60 inches (152 cm) of rainfall yearly while Los Angeles averages just under 15 inches (38 cm). Not only does the rainfall affect what plants will grow naturally, but it also impacts your ability to try plants that can tolerate the heat but need lots of water. They can survive in this instance in Los Angeles, but you'll have to add supplementary water to keep them alive. We'll talk about how much work you want to do in Chapter 3, but just keep in mind that this is a factor to consider.

For cold-climate gardeners, we have to think not just about rainfall but also snow and how that impacts the water resource. Minneapolis, Minnesota, and Breckenridge, Colorado, both reach subfreezing temperatures and have roughly the same annual average days of precipitation, but Breckenridge receives an average of 149 inches (379 cm) of snowfall each year whereas Minneapolis gets 52 inches (132 cm) of snow (and about double the amount of rain as Breckenridge). So even though both cities are technically the same growing zone, the distribution of precipitation is incredibly different and will impact plant growth with most of Breckenridge's falling in winter months.

If you live in an area with inconsistent or limited rain supply, consider rainwater harvesting techniques, such as having your gutters empty into barrels or buckets for later use. This sustainable practice is low cost, can be hidden from sight, and can keep your garden healthy even in times of drought.

Precipitation levels determine plant selection too. Though horsetails (*Equisetum hyemale*) can become invasive, they are also tolerant of very wet soils. In this modern garden, they are confined to a small area where they cannot spread. The area also collects rainwater, keeping it from turning into runoff.

The Native Question

A native plant is one whose species has been in your region for thousands of years and is considered a part of the natural flora. There is a lot of conversation around native plants and I'm not here to sway you one way or another. It's really a personal decision regarding how much you want to include these native plants in your garden, to what level you consider a plant native (to your county, state, country, or continent), and if you're comfortable using nativars. Nativars are cultivated selections of plants whose straight species is native. They often are propagated for mass distribution. Again, I'm not here to tell you which way to go, but I want to bring it up so that you can make the most informed decision for your yard.

There is limited research related to the impact of nativar varieties on pollinator and beneficial insects to date. The research that has been done has shown that there is little to no impact in most instances unless the cultivated native plant has had a dramatic change. For example, changing the flower or leaf color, creating a double flower, or having an adjusted flower shape that limits access to the pollen. If a nativar simply was introduced for longer flowering, a more compact size, or disease resistance, there seems to be low impact and it might be a good fit if you're looking for a more ecologically designed landscape. For more information on native plants and nativar research, see For More Inspiration on page 201.

This corner planting contains a combination of native plants, nativars, and introduced species, proving it's possible to create a beautiful planting with any combination.

These North American natives are at home in this Iowa garden. Including plants native to your region of the world can have many benefits, including providing habitat for wildlife and the fact that they're being accustomed to your local soil profile.

The Meaning of It

Okay, I'm sure you're asking yourself, "What does all of this mean?" I've been throwing around numbers and talking like a meteorologist, without a lot of direction. For the purposes of this picnic date, just make note of where your climate fits in all these instances:

- What are your temperature extremes?
- Are you more affected by cold or heat?
- Are you at an extreme elevation?
- How much and when do you receive your precipitation?
- How "native" do you want your garden to be?

These will continue to frame up your decision-making once we get to the plant recipes and combinations in Chapter 5.

Understanding your climate and your growing conditions is key to selecting the best plants for your landscape.

INVASIVE SPECIES

When you're choosing plants for your home, be certain that you're not including species that are considered invasive in your region. This refers to plants that will spread uncontrollably and take over the natural habitat. You may have heard of Japanese barberry, kudzu, buckthorn, or butterfly bush as plants that spread out of control; these are considered invasive in certain places, but not all.

If you are buying plants at your local garden center, there should be no worry about picking up an invasive plant. But if you're ordering online, be sure to do your research to avoid any issues. Even if the plant doesn't take over your yard, birds can pick up seed of invasive plants and spread it quickly. No one wants that.

For a list of plants that are deemed invasive, noxious, or prohibited in your region or state, consult your local university- or governmental-based agricultural program. If you live in the United States, the USDA has a fantastic resource available at www.invasivespeciesinfo.gov/subject/lists. Plant responsibly by not introducing an invasive plant to your neighborhood.

(CLOCKWISE) Common invasive plant species include the Japanese barberry, Japanese honeysuckle, purple loosestrife, and English ivy.

Happy Hour

DATE IDEA	***Cocktails on the patio***
DRINK	***Light + refreshing cocktail, glass of wine, or soda spritzer***
THE "WHY"	***Watching how light dances on your yard***

One of the most important things to know about your space is where, when, and how much sun is hitting your yard. This is one of the foundational pieces that will tell you what you can plant to see great results. When I first started gardening on my own, it was in a north-facing, middle unit townhome with a baby footprint of soil filled with roots from a poorly planted tree. We'll talk more about soil in a bit, but purely looking at the amount of sun my little patch of dirt received, it was pretty abysmal when my goal was to fill my garden with flowers and vegetables. You see, both of those things typically need at least 6 to 8 hours of sun exposure in my northern climate in Minnesota. Our growing seasons are fairly short, so we need those rays as much and as often as possible in our compacted season to push out the veggies and big, beautiful blooms. At my new home, the backyard faces south, so my gardening world has been turned upside down in the best of ways.

Figuring out how to classify your garden as Full Sun, Partial Sun, Partial Shade, Full Shade, or a combination thereof is not a one-time task. This is going to take some observation and some trial and error. Since it's such an important factor in seeing success in your garden, don't rush this step. Make it fun. Come with me on this journey and let's make a plan for scoping out the sun in your yard.

Spend time in your yard observing the movement of the sun. This collection of shade-loving plants thrives in this location because it receives only dappled sun.

LEVELS OF SUN EXPOSURE

This shady front garden proves that areas that receive only minimal light can still become beautiful gardens. The combination of astilbe, lenten rose, wild ginger, and ferns make a very pretty statement.

When you're plant shopping online or looking at plant tags in a garden center, you'll see different classifications of how much sun a plant needs to thrive. Remember that these are guidelines, and you'll want to take into account your regionality, elevation, and soil before making these a hard and fast rule.

FULL SUN For best results, these plants need at least 6 hours of sun, especially during the afternoon when the sun is at its most intense. Plants that are labeled Full Sun really need that heat and concentration of rays to stay healthy and produce at their maximum capacity, whether that's flowers, leaf color, fruits, or vegetables.

PARTIAL SUN Between 4 and 6 hours of sun is just about right for plants labeled as needing Partial Sun. They're not as needy as Full Sun plants, but still need the light to keep healthy. Especially in warmer climates, some of these plants may be more susceptible to heat damage or leaf burn with intense midday sun, so morning and afternoon sun exposure is a great way to keep this category going.

PARTIAL SHADE Similar to Partial Sun plants, those thriving in Partial Shade still require at least 4 hours of direct sunlight but do best when the exposure is limited to morning sun. For these plants, the east side of your house (or the west if you live in the Southern Hemisphere) or under a large tree that protects from afternoon sunlight will set you up for success.

FULL SHADE If a plant requires Full Shade, it doesn't mean it needs no sun. With very few exceptions, all plants need some access to sunlight but in varying degrees. Most Full Shade plants will do best planted on the north side of your house (or the south side if you live in the Southern Hemisphere) or under a tree canopy that offers filtered (or dappled) sunlight. Full Shade plants can handle some direct sunlight, but you definitely only want that direct hit in the morning or evening hours.

Dinner

DATE IDEA	***New dinner recipe + drink pairing***
DRINK	***Wine flights, nonalcoholic cocktail, sumac sparkler***
THE "WHY"	***Discussing the scope of your project***

Even though this is a dinner date, it's really an appetizer to Chapter 3, where we dig deeper into exactly what you're ready and willing to put into your design project. As you prep, pair, and taste your dinner, let's get to your *why.* What do you want out of this? Are you simply focused on a more beautiful front or backyard? Are you trying to create a functional entertaining space? Is your hope to build a pollinator garden to feed and protect the monarch butterflies on their migration?

For this final date at home, I'm going to navigate you through some conversation topics throughout the meal. I don't care if you're talking to yourself (no judgment here), talking with your partner, or bouncing ideas off family or friends, this is time for a little introspection. So, pick a new recipe or recipes, mix your drinks, or get out your wine tasting notes as you prep the food because we're about to dive into the first big conversation about your project!

It's important to consider what you plan to use your yard for before you start with the design process. This shady, elevated deck is perfect for relaxation.

Appetizers

Let's start light and fluffy and ease our way into the plan. Pop the lightest wine, pour the first sumac sparkler, or mix a bright nonalcoholic cocktail and start digging into why this yard project came up in the first place. Whether you just moved into a new house, want to give a tired landscape a facelift, or if you've got a project-specific need, now is when you get to really answer the *why*. It might be a simple answer or a combination of factors. Use these leading questions as conversation starters:

- What do I want the neighbors to say when they see my landscape?
- How long do I want to stay in this house?
- How do I use my yard now? How do I want to use it in the future?
- Are there any functional issues right now like water buildup, dark shady corners, patchy grass, overgrown weeds, etc.?

(OPPOSITE) Whether your outdoor area is big, like this one, or small, finding your "why" is important before you get started.

(RIGHT) Functionality matters in garden design. If you aren't steady on your feet, an uneven steppingstone path isn't a good choice. But if you or your kids don't mind an adventure, a walkway like the one passing through this side yard would be a fun addition.

Main Course

Now that you've thought a little deeper around the *why* behind why this is happening in the first place, I want you to start thinking about scope. Is this a garden bed in front or the sides of your house or are you putting in a pool and need to landscape the whole backyard? It's easy to see projects creep; once you start, you can't stop. So have the serious conversation now about where you want to start and stop. If the project is bigger than you want to bite off now, think about how to stage it over the coming years. Maybe take on the front flower beds now and then tackle a turf grass lawn replacement next year. Be realistic about the resources—time, energy, financial, and otherwise—you're willing to put in during your growing season before you make plans.

Before moving on, you also need consensus from everyone participating. Let me tell you, if I had my way, we would have no turf grass in my front or backyard. But my husband consistently reminds me that one reason we bought the new house was for our dogs to have space to run and play. Having that alignment and making the plan around the agreement is crucial not only for our marriage, but for the ultimate success of our project. These garden and landscaping projects are a big deal, so you don't want to do anything that could set them up to fail. All stakeholders have to be on board!

Be sure everyone in your household is on board before starting your project, not just with the hardscaping and plants, but also with any sheds or structures you'll need to add. These are all-hands-on-deck decisions!

Dessert

All right, now it's time to dig in and get serious: Let's talk money. Once you start talking plants, concrete, lumber, fire pits, etc., the money adds up quickly. We'll talk about some cost-saving tips in Chapter 3, but having a budget from the outset will really put up those guardrails. You know why you're doing this and have an idea of what you want to do, at least at a high level, so putting some dollars around it will really help you narrow things in as you pick plants and accessories. If you're working with a tighter budget, you're probably going to focus on smaller quantities of larger shrubs that will fill in and give you coverage. If you've got some extra money to spend, then we can start looking at layering seasonal plants such as collectible bulbs and masses of perennials combined with shrubs and trees. Both options can be stunning, but money talks and will play a role in what you choose in Chapter 5.

The dollars and cents aspect doesn't have to be challenging. Be realistic with what you've got to work with, and as we start combining your scope with your budget, we can make tweaks to get to your dream yard on budget with the additional resources at your disposal. As we move into more specific plans for your landscape, keep the notes from our at-home dates at the ready. You've spent a lot of time getting to know your space using a plant-focused lens. Now it's time to put them into action. See you on the other side!

If you're patient, you can save money over time by planting perennials that naturally multiply and can be divided, such as the hostas on this shaded slope.

Be realistic with your budget. Not everyone can make a grand statement like this homeowner. If your budget is smaller, opt for a pared-down version of this area; it will be just as beautiful.

3

Guardrails

"For every minute spent organizing, an hour is earned."

—BENJAMIN FRANKLIN

YOUR MOTIVATION to dig in the dirt may be to stay active, to spend time with your parents or kids outdoors, or to try your hand at growing your own food. You may just want a more beautiful backyard, deck, or front step. But at the end of the day, none of that matters to me. If you're ready to play with plants, I'm all on board to help you have success and create beauty in your own way.

First, we'll chat about why you even picked up this book in the first place. Then we can start to set boundaries around your design expectations and plant selections in Chapter 5. If you just want a beautiful backyard to entertain friends and family, let's find a more hard-working landscape plan. If you really want to make this part of your lifestyle and develop an evolving garden in which you add and subtract on a regular basis, we can broaden your palette a bit. Setting these expectations up front is going to reduce frustration at planting and concern over budget, and make sure that you really enjoy your space for the long run.

As we navigate this chapter together, we'll dig deeper into what you want to put into your landscape and what you want to get out of it. Since we've already talked about some basic (nongarden) design concepts and you've already gone on some dates with your garden, let's start asking what's next. It's easy to look at Instagram and Pinterest for ideas, but setting a budget, understanding the reality of living things in the landscape and the function of the plants in your setting will make sure that you create a stunning landscape for this year and the years to come. Remember, this is a long-term situation and not just for today!

As we start to establish some guardrails for this planting process and get closer to actually making some plant decisions, don't get too stressed because we haven't gotten into actual plant variety discussions yet. This is a slow burn, but well worth the wait. In this chapter, it's all about understanding what you actually want, both for inputs and outputs. Do you just want something that looks good every season, or do you want a botanical garden? Do you want to prune and fertilize once or twice, or do you want to *garden* garden? And how much do you want to spend? Let's kick this thing off!

Using plants as a natural barrier can allow you to carve out private space in your landscape for a reading nook, coffee corner, or quick cocktail outdoor lounge. Add plants with fragrance like roses (*Rosa spp.*) or Phenomenal Lavender (*Lavandula intermedia* 'Phenomenal') to make the space even more appealing.

The Enjoyment

Before we get into the nitty gritty of the *how* you're going to create your outdoor space, let's talk about *why*. If you don't have a clear understanding of *why* you're putting the time, energy, and money into the project, why start? The patio, deck, garden, and outdoor living rooms are meant to be enjoyed by your household, family, and friends. They're a place of respite and reflection. They're a showcase of your sweat equity and creativity. Gardens are places of hope and looking to the future. Remember the old high school English class acronym the 5Ws? Who, What, When, Where, and Why? That's what we need to tackle first.

Consider why you're creating this outdoor space—and who will be using it—before diving into the design. This garden boasts a lot of space to entertain guests, but maybe you prefer to grow vegetables or set up a play yard for your kids instead. Always keep your "why" in mind.

The "Why"

This is probably the most important moment in the whole book, so get ready. This is the time when all the details and planning and money go away. This is the reason you cracked open this book in the first place. It's time to take a moment with yourself and other decision makers in the household to talk about the reasoning behind doing your outdoor projects. I've broken down a few of the common themes I've heard over the years; take some time with each and see what resonates. And if it's none of these, take some time to reflect on your "why" and make sure that picture is clear in your head so the next steps in the planning process can be smooth and efficient. Laying this foundation will save you time, energy, and money in the long run.

BEAUTY. This is the most common answer I get when I ask why people are working on garden design projects. Of course, we want things to look beautiful, right? In a study done by my company Bailey Nurseries in 2020, three of the top four reasons people started gardening that year were focused on beautification and increased curb appeal. If your gut reaction says you're focused on beautifying your house and yard, I challenge you to take one step further. Are there certain areas that need some love? Is it because you spend more time in those areas or are there functional eyesores that need covering? Are you planting to increase curb appeal and your home's value for resale? That'll have a big impact on plant selection for immediate impact. Are

Finding your "why" could be as simple as wanting more beauty in your life, including right outside your own front door.

(OPPOSITE) Growing food is a functional consideration when designing your garden. This photo is proof that an edible garden can be both functional and beautiful.

you focused on beauty to create a more peaceful retreat from work and daily life? Answer the "why" for beauty by going one step deeper.

FUNCTION. The second most common answer I get is that people are doing garden or outdoor projects because it fulfills some sort of functional need. This sounds inorganic and hard, but I don't necessarily mean it that way. Function could be growing your own food or planting a hillside for erosion control. It might not be the sexiest "why," but it sure serves a purpose. Functional design also can mean hardscape installation for a fire pit or retaining wall, wetland restoration, planting for drought or wet soils, and weed suppression. In Chapter 2, you spent a lot of time with your yard. You found all the amazing things in the landscape and the challenges to overcome, so this is where you get to make the decision on what's really important. Do you have an area in your yard that stays wet until May? You might want to plant some shrubs like buttonbush or dogwood that thrive in wet conditions to soak up the early season water. Have really terrible soil? You might want to plant food crops that will help amend the soil over time. Function may not seem super sexy, but it can earn that title over time.

ACTIVITY. Gardening is work. We're going to talk about this in a few moments, but it's great exercise. You might be planning projects outside to get or stay active, either for yourself or your family. This is an absolutely valid—and fun—reason to get out there and get your hands dirty. In fact, the Centers for Disease Control and Prevention (CDC) has said that a little less than an hour of light yard work can burn over 300 calories. I don't know about you, but I'll take planting and weeding over the treadmill any day!

This homeowner overcame the challenges of a steeply sloped front yard by terracing it with layers of retaining walls planted with zone-specific choices.

ECOLOGY. One other common reason that people start gardening is to create a more sustainable, healthier ecosystem. Whether it's for water filtration or planting for pollinators, there are so many incredible benefits to getting plants in the ground. If ecological impact is your "why," you have incredible options that not only are great for the earth and pollinators but can be incredibly beautiful. Native plants are an increasingly important backbone of design and, while some may have a reputation for not being aesthetically pleasing, there are tons of native species and cultivated native plants that fit the bill. I will walk you through some fabulous plants, but if ecological design is your ultimate goal, I would also highly recommend reading Kelly Norris's book *New Naturalism*. It's a great next step after finishing this book to coach you through specific steps in ecological horticulture and plant matrix plant design.

To continue sewing the common thread throughout the book, there's no wrong answer to your "why." As you've probably gleaned from me, I don't live in a world of absolutes, so I've picked a number of reasons from the lists above. And that's okay, but still be sure to narrow your focus a bit to understand your central reasoning. Mine was a focus on function with a close second of beauty. What's yours?

Including native plant species in your garden encourages a more diverse ecosystem and offers benefits to many other living beings beyond the resident humans.

Today vs. the Future

How you enjoy your space may change and evolve over time. Kids may come into the picture (your own or those of family and friends). You may move. You may plant a tree or have one that that dies and changes the sun exposure. Life happens, and sometimes we can't predict it, but our goal is to do our best. In this planning, we want to think about how our outdoor space will be enjoyed over time. Plants take time to settle in and live up to their full potential. Hey, not unlike most of us, right? We have to consider today *and* tomorrow. And when we're talking trees, that means 20 years from now.

Seasonality

Making note of when you plan to utilize and enjoy your outdoor space is also important as you start to think of the plants that you'll put in the ground. Thinking about how your family schedule affects time at home, your travel lifestyle, your emotional connection to certain plants, and understanding the possibilities of multi-season planting all play a role in your design approach. It's not just about what looks good in a garden center today, or what looks really nice in a picture online, but getting to know plants and how they change over time in connection with how you plan to experience the garden is key.

LIFESTYLE. Like we'll talk about shortly with the work inputs in the garden, understanding when you'll use the space based on your and your family's lifestyle should impact your ultimate design. Just like any other home decision, you've got to account for all the other pieces of your busy life. You're not going to buy a sports car as your only vehicle if you've got four kids, so why plan a garden with summer-blooming plants if you're going to be at the baseball diamond or lake house at that time of year? There are too many amazing plants that can show off when your lifestyle allows you to be home to enjoy them. As we continue narrowing the guardrails to your unique planting design, consider these leading questions and keep track as we move into the next couple of chapters:

- What time of year are you home most regularly? Of that time, when would you hope to be outside enjoying your yard?
- If you have children, at what time of year are they most busy with activities?
- Do you like to host friends, family, or colleagues at your house? Are there certain seasons or times of day when you might be outdoors during your hosting experience?
- Are there certain times of year that you travel, either for a quick weekend getaway or for a more extended period of time? Remember that plants need water and food, just like us, so if you're going to be gone, we've got to choose plants that can handle that stress without concern. And again, you don't want to plan an early spring-blooming garden if you're going to be at your warm beach house before returning home in June.
- Think about your day-to-day life. Are you a homebody or someone who likes to be out and about? Do you enjoy working on home projects or prefer home to be a place of rest?

Consider each of these, and any other related questions, as you determine how you'll enjoy your yard. There are no wrong answers, but the

more you sort through all these questions now, the better off you'll be as you choose your design style and pick plants.

EMOTION. There's nostalgia around plants. Whether it's picking berries with grandma, pruning rose bushes with mom, or the scent of lilacs wafting in through your childhood window, most everyone can think of a connection to the garden. This relationship with plants and the outdoors may seem like an afterthought when choosing plants, but I think this is such an important piece of design. Gardens are a place of deeply personal decisions, great pride, and a sense of immense accomplishment. Including plants that mean something to you deepens that connection to your space and allows you to tell the story of your landscape in a more intimate way. Think back to your childhood and young adult years. I distinctly remember picking blueberries as a young boy with my grandma Marcia at our cabin in northern Minnesota. To this day I bake blueberry cake in memory of those days. And every time I make it, I tell the story (probably *ad nauseum* to my husband) about how grandma and I would clamber over the rocks to find the best blueberry bushes to make blueberry cake and pancakes. I remember jumping rope with my great-grandma Margaret in front of her house when she was in her 90s. She sat among her favorite pink roses (now introduced by Easy Elegance Roses as Grandma's Blessing rose in her honor), laughing and cheering us on. These memories are seared into our brains and elicit such strong emotion that we absolutely should bring them into our new landscapes. Every time I give a tour of my garden, I make sure to point out the Grandma's Blessing rose and tell people

Gardens change and evolve over time as plants grow and your life changes. Think about what your new space will look like in 1, 5, or 10 years' time as you are planning.

If you are away from your home certain times during the year, whether it's because of travel, kids' sports, or whatever, don't create a garden that is at its peak at that time. Or one that requires a lot of work when you're not going to be around.

about Margaret Bailey. It's a connection to my past by creating something special today and for the future. It's a unique and special way to celebrate memory in the living art that is your garden. What elicits memories for you? Smells, colors, flowers, or a combination thereof? Think of your favorite stories and jot them down so we can be sure to include those special memories in your landscape plan.

FOUR SEASONS. Gardening isn't just for one season. It's not just for when things are blooming in the garden center in spring or for the gorgeous yellow, orange, and red of fall. It's not just for the

Certain plants elicit emotions from us, thanks to memories we may have of a person or place from our past. This hydrangea planting at Heritage Museums & Gardens on Cape Cod oozes with nostalgia, which can help inform plant choices.

colors of summer or container arrangements of winter. It's all of that together in the same design plan. We are so conditioned to think of plants at the moment in time we see them showcased on social media or in a magazine that we forget how they change over time and interact with the other plants in the landscape. I won't stay on my soapbox too long because we'll talk more about designing for a multi-season garden in Chapter 4, but as you think about how you'll enjoy the garden, think about what seasons are most important to you. It can be influenced by your lifestyle or emotions, absolutely, but how do you want to see that transition of season play out in your backyard? There are so many fabulous plants that can add multiple seasons of interest that may get overlooked or only featured for one season of splendor. Think of something like a red-twigged dogwood (*Cornus sericea*) that you might recognize in winter or holiday decorative pot displays. You know, those great red stems that brighten up the evergreen boughs and shine against the snow? Well, there are some fabulous varieties like Neon Burst™ dogwood that not only have red stems in winter, but white flowers in spring, chartreuse leaves in summer, and fabulous sunset shades of orange and red in fall. Talk about a hardworking plant that delivers all the goods! Again, off my soapbox, but think about making your garden a showplace throughout the year and not just with tulips in spring or hydrangeas in summer. It can be so much more.

Planting for four seasons can keep your garden looking and feeling alive, even in the winter.

The Work

Before we get too far, let me start by acknowledging that creating and maintaining a beautiful landscape is work. I don't care if you're hanging a couple of flower baskets or planting a half-acre lot from scratch, it's going to take some sweat equity (not to mention financial equity). Having a gorgeous green lawn and full, colorful flower beds takes some commitment. Now, I'm not saying all of this to scare you away. I mean, you're in Chapter 3, so you're committed to this whole garden design idea, but I want to be realistic and set the right expectations. There's lots of room to make decisions that impact your short- and long-term inputs into your green space. There absolutely are plants that are easier to maintain, and for those who want to live in the garden a bit more for a respite from your busy life, I've got some more particular combinations that will take a bit more finesse and attention. Just remember that at the end of the day, plants are living things that need some nurturing and loving care, but there are levels of caring and maintenance that factor into your decision-making as you start to choose plants in Chapter 5. I'm all about helping you create beauty, no matter where on that spectrum of inputs you live today.

I'm not going to sugarcoat it: Gardens need someone to care for them. And sometimes, being that someone isn't easy. Don't bite off more than you can chew by creating a huge garden if you aren't ready for it. Small spaces are just as lovely. You can always expand later.

Social Media vs. Reality

One of the challenges we all run up against in many aspects of our lives is the false reality of social media. There's a sense of aspiration to the perfectly curated images we scroll through every day. And there's a place for that. It can drive our curiosity, inspire our creativity, and open doors to new learning. If we accept that for what it is, we're starting from a good place. While this may hit home in more than one area of your life, let's not get too philosophical and just focus on the inspiration behind creating a beautiful outdoor living space and garden.

You can read all your favorite magazines (who are edited by some of my favorite people), scroll through a highly curated social feed of one of your favorite plant brands (I'm the guy behind a couple of those), or drool over the gardens of world-class designers (same) and be completely inspired but have no idea how to make that a reality at your house. However, that curiosity is what will drive great design. Understand that in most of those instances, there are crews of people who work hard to get that one perfect shot. So, when you're looking at that inspirational image, step back and think of how it relates to your aesthetic and home, just like you did during your dates in Chapter 2.

- What captured your attention about the photo in the first place?
- What colors draw you in? What about color combinations?
- How does the image make you feel?
- Are there shapes that echo lines in your existing hardscape or home?

What is it about this space that draws you in? Or doesn't draw you in, as the case may be? When coming across a photo of an outdoor area you like, take note of what's appealing to you.

- Are there any patterns that you'd like to replicate at your house?
- Do you see plants, big or small, that would fill any of your specific space constraints?
- Do you find any plants that would be a great focal point or interesting talking feature in your yard?

We all understand that what we see on social media isn't necessarily something we can copy-paste into our lives. Use these questions to continue homing in on design themes that you'd like to bring to life at home. Use this tool to add to your checklists. Look at the post's description to see if the specific plant names are listed. If not, comment or send a DM to whomever posted and ask, even if they're a big designer or a national magazine. Shoot your shot—you never know who might respond! Even if you can't replicate the intricate design of someone like Piet Oudolf or Kelly Norris, your reality can be incredibly beautiful and personal with their inspiration. As I was learning the basics of plant ID, I asked a million questions. To this day, one of my favorite things is to walk new gardens with the homeowner or another plant person and find at least one plant that is new to me. Who knows, maybe that'll be you one day? And your landscape will become the one inspiring others on social media (and, of course, in person).

Short- and Long-Term Effort

No pain. No gain. I'm not one for sports metaphors or overexertion—I literally had sore muscles after weed whacking the overgrown grass at my new house—but working in the yard is one of those really great post-workout burns where you can actually see the difference before and after. Maybe I shouldn't admit how feeble my arms were that day, but it's all to say that if I can do it, anyone can. As we set the guardrails around how much effort you want to put in your yard, you've got to look at the short-term pains for the long-term gains. Weed whacking that overgrown grass, while painful that night, made it so much easier to lay bed lines and plant my hillside so that it never needed to be mowed again; no more pushing the lawn mower up a steep incline!

As we start to work on actually designing your outdoor space in Chapters 4 and 5, remember that you can tackle it in one of two ways: Set the goal first and work backwards, or set boundaries for your inputs and let that dictate your end result. When you're thinking about short- and long-term effort inputs (we'll talk financial in a bit), focus on a few key topics: human capital, tools, and maintenance.

The use of groundcovers and container plantings can reduce maintenance and selecting plants that thrive in your climate and soil will further simplify the care needs of your garden.

HUMAN CAPITAL. Do you have friends and family who will help you plant? Can you order some pizza and fill a cooler with drinks to entice people to dig in the dirt? Planting small annuals and perennials is a pretty quick task (think 1 plant per minute per person), but larger shrubs and trees adds some time because the hole has to be bigger, you might have to dig around rocks or bad soil or need someone to stabilize the top (think 1 plant per 5 minutes per person). Some quick math will tell you if you can do it alone or if you'll need an army to get everything planted.

TOOLS. Friends can bring shovels, but are you building a new retaining wall or deck? Putting in irrigation or adding a fence? Make sure to think

All gardens require some input to maintain them, some more than others. Keep this key factor in mind when determining how grand of a scale you want to shoot for.

wholistically and not just about the plants themselves. Little evening projects can quickly turn into weekend projects, so be sure you're thinking ahead about the tools needed to get the project done. If you don't have everything yourself, can you rent or hire it out? What does that do to your timeline and budget? Be as organized as possible to make the installation run smoothly.

MAINTENANCE. Once you get the plants and landscape installed, you've got to maintain it to keep it gorgeous. They're living things, remember? Think about your lifestyle today and in the years to come. Do you have an hour a week to get your hands dirty, or do you want to make this an ongoing hobby where you relax by working in the garden after work most days? Be realistic about how your future may change with work, family, travel, and other hobbies. There's no Magic 8 Ball that can predict everything, but do your best so that all this time, effort, and money being spent today doesn't go to waste tomorrow.

There's no one answer to this question of effort. Committing to an hour a week doesn't mean your outdoor space will look any less amazing than someone spending an hour a night. It's about choosing the right plants for the right place with the right intention. Being thoughtful now will bring you more success in the future.

Gardens with a lot of walls, walkways, water features, and other hard-scaping often require hiring a contractor. However, there are plenty of ways around that if you prefer to go the DIY route.

DIY vs. Contractor

Deciding if you're going to take on the project yourself (or with family and friends) or hiring it out can be a big decision. Digging in the dirt yourself can give an immense amount of satisfaction and ownership over the project, but you truly might just not have the time or capability to do everything the project requires, and you may need to bring in a contractor.

When I started planting the gardens at my new house, it was a fully DIY experience. Not only could I not afford a contractor (I bought a house, got married, installed a fence, and had a half-acre to plant all within one year), but I wanted to grow the outdoor space in phases with my own hands. I wanted to lay the foundation of the outdoor space myself so I could make it special and unique. I wanted to be able to tell stories about each plant and rock and piece of art when I hosted dinner parties. These things were important to me, and I had the great support of friends and family to help make that dream a reality.

DIY Pros Flexibility, personalized touch, no labor budget, and intimate knowledge of each outdoor space.

DIY Cons Projects take much longer, might require reshaping of beds and hiring contractors in the future to redo hardscaping, and potentially limited scope due to technical expertise.

Contractor Pros Quick and efficient, able to take on larger projects, and deeper well of knowledge.

Contractor Cons More expensive, less connection to the design, and at the whim of the contractor's labor.

If life is wild and crazy, you're working under a tight timetable, or have a larger project ahead of you, bringing in a contractor might be the best bet. If you're not a plumber, probably don't try installing an irrigation system or water feature. If you're wanting to wire in a sound system, probably don't do the electrical work yourself. Hire the professionals to do their job, and fit in work where you have the capacity, skillset, and interest.

Like so much of this, there's not one right answer to how you execute your project. Take these factors, and those to follow, into consideration before you stick a shovel in the ground. If you're anything like me, you'll probably end up with some sort of hybrid approach. Hire out contractors when you're able to for the bigger chunks and then plant the plants yourself. Whichever way you go, weigh your options, and make the best decision for you and your household.

The Spend

OK, talking about spending money on your garden might not be the most relaxing and easy conversation, but it's important as we work our way into actually designing your outdoor space. Because it all flows back to the money, right? You can DIY and work your tail off, but it still costs money for that landscaping stone, irrigation tubes, and plant material. I'll be super up front in that I'm not great at money. Well, I take that back. I'm really good at spending money, but not so great at saving or planning for it. So, this is an area that I've needed help organizing over the years. Thank goodness I married a money-conscious planner. If you're anything like me, you should begrudgingly pay attention as we talk about planning for this investment in your property, and always remember, this is an investment and not just an expense.

This chapter is all about setting guardrails. We're here to set some boundaries around what you can and cannot do, at least for right now. I'm not one who loves to hear no or have a limit on the extent of my projects, but then reality sets in and those boundaries end up being a great thing. Having constraints pushes creativity, forces you to figure out what is truly most important, and makes impossible decisions a reality. When the limit doesn't exist and the world is my oyster, I am really good at making major plans. Then I take the step back and look at available resources, and I'm forced to assess the practicality of my ideas. I like to start big and pare down from there and I would challenge you to do the same. Dare to dream a little bit. That's where such great inspiration can begin. We can always cut back, but adding layers to a weak foundation never ends well.

As you're approaching your landscape plans, dream with me. Let's focus on the wants first and then we'll drill down to the needs. What have you always dreamed about? A cedar fence, in-ground pool, and lush landscaping like we only see in the movies? A woodland oasis that simply oozes calm and quiet? An ultra-chic, modern hedge row around your Miami-style mansion? Remember, we're not quite living in reality yet. Close your eyes and allow yourself to drift. Take a snapshot in your brain of what that dreamscape looks like. Think back to Chapter 2 and the lessons you learned about looking for color, texture, shape, etc. What did your dreamscape look like? This is going to help set the foundation for our budget process. Start big and cut back as needed. Build that heavy foundation and add the accents that make sense for you. As we dig deeper, keep in mind the general rule of thumb that landscape costs can average about 10 to 15 percent of your home's value. Again, that's a generalization that can absolutely go up or down based on your goals for the outdoor space, but if you're looking for somewhere to start, you can use that calculation.

While it's good to dream a little, it's also good to keep your feet on the ground. Even if you're just starting with a small front yard planting so you can stick to your budget, plan for beautiful, long-term results you can build on when time and money allow.

Materials

Landscaping is not for the faint of heart. It's not the cheapest hobby, nor is it the most inexpensive remodeling project you will do. The cost of goods is what it is, but I'll help you navigate where you need to spend money and where you can find creative solutions.

PLANTS. I'm being very honest here. Plants are expensive. I've had my own sticker shock when walking around a garden center. But allow me to take you a little bit behind the curtain to learn how plants come to market. New varieties that are improvements to what is already available can come to be through a couple general avenues: natural mutations (in a good, non-Frankenstein's monster kind of way) are discovered in the wild or intentional breeding is done to target specific plant attributes. In either case, a significant amount of money is invested to introduce this new variety that solves an existing problem: better disease resistance, longer flowering time, more heat or cold tolerance, smaller stature, stronger flower color, etc. This can mean millions of dollars of research, trials, and marketing. Beyond all that, simply growing a plant from a seed or a cutting to a container size sold in a garden center can take three to five years. That's a lot of input costs to get a plant to the retail floor. It takes a heck of a lot to get them ready for sale. None of this is to come off as preachy as a kid who works for a nursery, but just to give some context since we're talking money.

Different categories of plants will come at different price points. Going for the cheapest option may not always get you the desired result, so understanding what you're buying and what it'll do in the landscape is really important.

Annuals are useful for adding quick color to a planting or container.

Perennials return year after year so while they are more expensive than annuals, they provide many seasons of color and interest.

Annuals, or plants that are intended to survive only one growing season, are typically the least expensive option. They're the quickest for growers to bring to market and will generally be a smaller size so the cost structure fits the product. Annuals bring bright pops of color and unique pops of texture to the landscape and decorative pots. You may also find beautiful hanging baskets of premade containers at garden centers filled with fabulous annual plants. With annuals, think of petunias, marigolds, begonias, pansies, and snapdragons. Positive: generally low cost in comparison to other categories and have big garden impact. Downside: these plants only last one season and then they have to be pitched.

Perennials are plants that come back year after year, but generally have green or softer shoots and don't develop woody stems. Common perennials include daylilies, hostas, catmint, ornamental onion, lavender, sedum, and ornamental grasses such as Karl Foerster feather reed grass, fescue, autumn moor grass, Japanese forest grass, purple fountain grass, and pampas grass. In terms of budget, perennials are middle of the road. You might have a little bit of sticker shock, especially if you're buying a smaller container that you'd expect to be low budget, but remember all the work that it takes to get these plants to the garden center *and* that they'll come back year after year, so it's a great investment in an established landscape or container garden. Where annuals give that pizzaz to the garden, perennials give the beginning of consistency that you'll remember year after year. Seasonal color and texture, reliable return to the landscape, and massive diversity in plants make perennials a garden favorite. Where annuals give the oooh to the garden, perennials give the ahhh.

Shrubs and trees are the backbone of a garden. Select them carefully because they'll be there for many, many years.

After the oooh and ahhh are done, it's time for the wow! Shrubs and trees are the bedrock of your landscape. They are the structure that allows the freedom of perennials and annuals to fill in the gaps with such amazing beauty. This can be everything from hydrangeas and roses to maple trees and ginkgo. This is the category that is going to hit your bank account the hardest. Shrubs and trees take a long time to produce, so the costs are inherently higher. Remember that these plants will live in your landscape for years, and many times for decades. There is a white oak tree in the backyard of my family home that has been there for over 100 years. Talk about bang for your buck . . . trees and shrubs are where it's at. This might be an investment over time, but the payoff is massive. Remember this is what everything else is built around, so it's worth spending the extra money to do it right. When you're shopping in the garden center, you'll see shrubs and trees in different size containers with corresponding prices. If you're willing to wait a bit for the plants to fill in— remember, these will take a number of years to reach their mature size—you can save a few bucks and start small. If you're hoping to see some quicker turnaround in the next few years, budget and plan for bigger containers so you've got some immediate impact and faster establishment to put on some size. Think of it this way: When you're making updates to your house, the flooring and appliances are some of the big-ticket items, but you have to do it because everything else follows their style. Same with shrubs and trees. They're the big stuff and the perennials and annuals are the dish towels, paint color, and cabinet pulls. They are equally important and give so much personality to the space but come at different price point levels.

Tulips and other flowering bulbs add a pop of color to this urban front garden. They are inexpensive and fun additions to your garden.

Other categories of plants include bulbs, tubers, and seeds. These will generally be on the lower cost side, near annuals, unless you're going for super exotic plants. Seeds are fantastic if you're planning an edible or pollinator garden. They're inexpensive and relatively easy to sow for a beautiful crop later in the season. Bulbs and tubers are more seasonal plants that require just a bit of extra work but are generally lower cost. With this category, think daffodils, tulips, calla lilies, hyacinth, and even potatoes. While some may require a bit of extra work if they're not hardy for your climate, they're a fantastic way to bring life to your garden in a season that may otherwise be bare, and they're a great way to save a few bucks. If you like to plant bulbs in massive quantities like I do to create swaths of color, that might push you into the shrub-level spending, but oh my goodness is it worth it. Think of a sea of grape hyacinths in spring that literally creates the illusion of a blue river running through your yard. Delicious.

HARDSCAPING. I just talked about shrubs and trees being the foundation of your landscape, but you can't forget the hardscaping elements that make up the base of your design. We'll get into usage in the next chapter, but wrapping your head around costs for this material is a great starting point. Plants can be expensive, but hardscaping takes it to a whole new level. From retaining walls to water features and patios, these hard surfaces create entertaining spaces, delineate space, and establish character. When you're thinking of budget, hardscape materials are going to be a heavier investment and they can help determine the scope and timeline for your projects. If you don't have the budget to put in the full fire pit with pavers right now, then maybe you start with just plants and some

edging along your fence line. If you have a hillside where you need to create a walkway for safety reasons, start with the staircase and budget other items afterwards.

I'm writing about these examples because this is my exact scenario at the new house, but hopefully they ring true to you as well. Taking a phased approach made the most sense for us since we've had so many other costs in buying the new house. It's the hardest thing for me to do because, as you can probably gather, I'm not the most patient person in the world. I want everything right away. Instant gratification at its finest. But resources are not unlimited, so using hardscaping as the budget guardrails helped prioritize our project list.

Other hardscaping items to consider when you're looking at your project costs are driveways or walking paths, BBQs or outdoor kitchens, pergolas, decks or patios, and pads around a pool. These pieces can really swing you away from that 10 to 15 percent of value pretty quickly, so bear that in mind as you go through the process. This isn't about saying no; it's just about setting expectations and making a plan.

IRRIGATION. This may not be the sexiest topic in the book, but it can be crucial for the success of your outdoor space. Now, I know that this can be tricky based on where you live. Water restrictions and being water conscious is super important, so be aware of your local guidelines when planning for irrigation. I'll touch on water usage and impact on future dollars spent in a moment, but for now we're just focused on the up-front budget. If you are in a position where irrigation makes sense and is reasonable for your climate, this is another one of those potentially big-ticket items, especially if you're planning to irrigate your turf lawn. There are a ton of factors that impact this cost, such as permit fees, contractor costs, scope of project, drip irrigation versus turf irrigation, automatic versus manual systems, watering zones, and so on, but at least this can give you a starting point from which to build a plan.

LABOR. I tend to get excited when I look at materials pricing online and think, "oh, that's not too bad." I calculate the cost of pavers and lay out a plan and smile with anticipation. I planned to build a fire pit under the tree canopy at my new house. Well, getting the materials wasn't too bad, but then I read about all the tools I'd need to install it properly, how many people I'd need to get it done, and the time to set aside. I just didn't have the capacity, nor did it make financial sense once I had to add in the tool rental. As I was budgeting, I realized it would be more efficient to hire a crew to help. So, unless you have tools at home and a group of family and friends to help, some of the bigger projects are better left to the professionals. Especially if it's related to plumbing or electrical. Be smart. Save money where you can, but hiring those that do it best up front is going to save you in the long run and keep you safe. And, if you're lucky enough to have a plumber or electrician in the family, see if they'll accept a case of their favorite beverage for payment. You never know, right?

(OPPOSITE) Hardscaping, which includes walkways, patios, decks, retaining walls, and the like, can be among the most costly aspects of a planting plan.

(NEXT SPREAD) The right hardscaping can make or break a project. From the materials used to their style and color, put some thought into the process.

Some gardens require more labor to install and maintain than others. Don't be fooled into thinking gardens like this moss-covered beauty won't require at least some maintenance.

MAINTENANCE. You get everything in, you're loving life, and then . . . a tree branch falls on your new retaining wall and breaks a few bricks. Cue the baby crying emoji. Something always happens, doesn't it? When we bought our new house, it had all new appliances, and within a month one of the shelves inside the refrigerator just shattered out of nowhere. How does that even happen? But it does, so we have to budget and plan for ongoing maintenance and repairs. Remember that this can be a substantial investment, so just like your car or your siding, the plants and hardscaping need some annual love too.

In addition to tree branches damaging your beautiful retaining wall, you'll want to plan an annual plant budget. Things die, squirrels dig up bulbs, annuals need replacing, mulch needs a refresh. One of the joys of gardening is that it's a living landscape that is always changing. That also means you've got to help it along with a refresh, which comes with a price tag. It doesn't have to be huge, but you don't want all that hard work going to waste in year two or three if certain plants struggle in their new homes in the garden or if you want to fill in a bit more to create a more dense or multi-season space. Now, I know it seems callous to say that "things die," but it's true. I've said it a number of times in this book, but it's worth a reminder: Plants are living things. These aren't the plastic, dust-collecting green things in your doctor's waiting room. Sometimes they get too much sunlight or water, or maybe a pest or disease attacked the plant and it couldn't survive. Instead of mourning the loss or feeling frustrated, you could take a slightly different approach. Try to figure out what went wrong and then look at it as an opportunity to try something new. Of course, this comes with a cost, but that's why we budget for plants every year!

Plants are living things and sometimes they die. Taking care of a pretty landscape like this one comes with lots of life lessons.

Budget Planning

Now that we've got an idea of some of the areas you'll need to include in the budget, it's time to dive in. If this isn't your favorite thing to do, pour a glass of wine and turn on your favorite music in the background. Let's make it fun and think of all the beauty you're going to create!

Remember all those pages ago where I asked you to date your space? Well now it's time to start looking back at those notes to determine what gets you excited and will make you fall in love with your outdoor space. We're going to start moving down the funnel from all the things you love and start making them a bit of a reality. So, bust out your Home Date Checklists and let's get to work! Sorry to be bossy. First child syndrome. But we've got budgets to plan!

Let's start with your top five takeaways from your home dates. What really inspired you? Was it a cool fence? A unique plant combination? A piece of garden art? Think back to what got you most excited as you were learning more about your home and outdoor space. Then think about the needs of the space that you learned. Do you need better drainage? Full sun plants? A retaining wall? An outdoor entertainment area? Start making a wants vs. needs list. Put together a list or spreadsheet and be sure to leave room for a budget column. Write out everything that you'd like to do without consequence. If you want a pool and it *could* work for your yard, write it down. If you want all yellow plants, go for it. If you want a limestone patio, add it to the list.

Maybe a new deck or waterfall is not in your initial plans due to budget constraints, but that doesn't mean they won't eventually find their way into your backyard. Keep a list of your dreams and then work toward making them happen over time.

Then make a check in the want or need column. Based on available resources, what can you bite off now versus save for future years? I'm sorry to bring up a phased approach again, but it is the responsible thing to do when you're working on a budget (thanks for drilling this into my thick skull, mom!).

Since we're not into actual design yet, this is just going to be a starting point. This chapter is all about guardrails, so we're still living a bit in the gray and not total black and white, but as you narrow down your list from wants to needs based on presumed costs, that will at least help you decide if you're putting in the fire pit this year or if you're just focusing on plant material to add some vitality to your space, and then adding more hardscaping next year. Bit by bit, we'll get you to the yard of your dreams.

As you work through this process, remember to get multiple quotes and think creatively as you approach budget. There are always ways to find hidden dollars. Whether that's upcycling old railroad ties instead of installing stone steppers or shopping off-season for hardscaping materials and plants, you can earn some significant savings. Don't be scared to price shop, ask neighbors for plant swaps on cool divided perennials and bulbs, and check estate sales for unique garden art or tools. One other thing to remember when plant shopping is to pay special attention to each plant's mature size, especially with shrubs and trees. Just because it's small in the pot now doesn't mean it'll stay like that over time. We'll talk more about spacing later on, but as you budget, remember that shrubs and trees (and some bigger perennials) can take up large amounts of space in the landscape. They might be more expensive than smaller perennials, annuals, or seed, but you need fewer of them because they will fill in over time. This is one instance where patience truly is a virtue worth striving for, especially as it affects your wallet.

My final comment on budget is that you need to think beyond the installation budget. I'm not talking about maintenance anymore, but the savings from decisions you make today. I'm a glass half full kind of guy, so let's look at the positives of spending money up front. You may spend a bit more on drip irrigation now, but in the long run you'll use less water—yay for sustainability—and reduce your ongoing costs. You might spend a chunk of money buying plugs of grasses or perennials to replace an area of turf, but if you buy the right product, then you're not having to re-seed, water, fertilize, and de-thatch your lawn regularly. That's time and money saved!

This aspirational outdoor living room may not be in your budget today, but maybe a smaller stone fireplace with a seating area is.

4

Designing Your Space

"You can't use up creativity. The more you use, the more you have."

—MAYA ANGELOU

NOW THAT WE'VE GOTTEN the budget conversation out of the way, let's have some fun! I've been telling you for the last three chapters that we would get to the designing and plant selection, and we're there! All that foundational information is really important and will help shape your selections in this chapter. We're going to start with some high-level design profiles that will frame up design concepts and plant choices. Based on what you learned about your property, your style, and how much work you want to do in the last three chapters, you'll start to see where you fit. The puzzle pieces are starting to come together!

To give some context to making material selections, I've given personalities to three different design styles that are most prevalent in today's landscapes. Of course, there are others, and you might find that you're drawn to a combination of these personalities, and that's totally fine. You don't have to live in a black and white world of absolutes. I sure don't; I live in full color, baby! There are no hard and fast rules that you *have* to abide by, but starting from the same place makes sure we're all talking the same language. Let's meet our friends Martha, Tommy, and Kelly!

MARTHA
The Classic

Refined style. Intentional design. Functional approach.

We're going to start with a design style that is likely familiar to many of us. Martha has a refined style that is legible, intentional, and functional. This classic approach mixes bulbs, annuals, perennials, shrubs, trees, and likely vegetables into the design in a way that is easy to maintain but brings fabulous color to the landscape in all four seasons. The planting pattern is articulate and not overdone, leaving some room to breathe while not looking bare. Martha is the hostess with the mostest, so having something to shine in the garden all year-round is important. Also, when she's having guests, it's a fun party trick to showcase what's growing in the garden by incorporating the edible plants into cocktails and the meal. Who doesn't love dinner and a show?

When I talk about this classic design style, I don't want you to think boring or cliché. This might be a landscape you see in a suburban neighborhood, but one that you drive by and comment on how nice it is. Martha is not basic. She is classic. And that is beautiful and stunning and can mix in a lot of really unique plants, infuse personality, and be highly functional at the same time. Martha may have a mix of styles in her landscape, but it's all about refinement, ease of maintenance, and being a productive garden. By that, I mean that the garden gives back with fruits and vegetables, cut ornamental flowers, has pollinator-friendly plants for bees and other insects, and provides that seasonal color I mentioned. Martha figures that if we're going to put the time and money into the garden, we should get something back from it beyond just being pretty. And I can get on board with that!

(OPPOSITE) A classic Martha front garden design offers style, beauty, and personality while still being functional.

(RIGHT) The Martha style might include edible plants or cut flowers in the design but in a refined, potager-esque style that is beautiful and productive.

While this might be on a larger scale than most home gardens, it captures Martha's spirit with classic plant species such as panicle hydrangeas (*Hydrangea paniculata*), ninebark (*Physocarpus opulifolius*), feather reed grass (*Calamagrostis acutiflora*), and Russian sage (*Salvia yangii*). Building garden beds with legible swaths of color and texture are characteristic of this design style.

This classic style may use masses of the same cultivar, or variety, of plants to have a dramatic affect and be paired with complementary colors throughout the seasonal progression. Think a gorgeous hydrangea hedge planted along the foundation of the house with a mix of flowering perennials and ornamental grasses in front. Martha may also have a cottage garden feel where she uses more traditional hardscaping and classic plants such as roses and colorful perennials for pollinators and cut flower arrangements. Or Martha may plant layered hedges around her back patio to create a more intimate outdoor space for hosting dinners or BBQs. They all bring beauty and function to an otherwise bland landscape.

Again, to avoid cliché or stereotype, my intention is not for Martha to seem like a *Leave It to Beaver* character or Stepford wife. That persona belongs nowhere in this profile. Martha is a busy working woman who appreciates the balance of having friends over after a long week. She works hard to have a gorgeous space to host, and so she wants the outdoors to match everything she's putting into it. She chose tough but beautiful plants so she can have a gorgeous landscape without being out there every day to maintain it. Martha is badass.

Cutting flowers from the garden for dinners or date nights on the patio is quintessential Martha. Every plant in this arrangement came straight from the backyard. The pastel colors of Endless Summer The Original hydrangea (*Hydrangea macrophylla* 'Bailmer') and phlox (*Phlox paniculata*) are beautifully accented by the neutral green tones of spirea (*Spiraea betulifolia*), shrubby cinquefoil (*Potentilla fruticosa*), and Ivory Halo dogwood (*Cornus alba* 'Bailhalo').

TOMMY
The Minimalist

Clean lines. Tidy boxes. Fashion over function.

Clean, sharp edges, repetition, and a tempered color palette are all hallmarks of the Tommy design style.

Tommy's modern design aesthetic is one of minimalism and repetition. Tommy keeps the focus on a streamlined color palette, natural tones, structure, and the use of lines to direct the eye. As we begin to move those same patterns to the outdoor space, it gives us a framework to start building the plan for the outdoor living space and landscape.

Remember that as we discuss design, it's not just about the garden, but rather the entire outdoor space in which you'll live. The outdoor room is especially important in Tommy's world.

Before any design project, you have to understand the function of the space. Will you be hosting clients or colleagues? Will it be a family

Modern design aesthetics use lines and patterns to draw the eye through the landscape.

space? Is it a reflective retreat from the chaos of daily life? Light, texture, materials, patterns, and color all play an important role in setting the mood. Everything is placed intentionally and should elicit emotion. The power of design is impactful on all of those who encounter it, leaving lasting memories, feelings, and snapshots that represent the owner.

One of the things that I love about Tommy's modern aesthetic is the ability to move someone through the space in a seemingly effortless way. Creating pathways with lines, manmade or natural. Adding swaths of ornamental grass that provide structure with slight movement as the wind picks up on an autumn evening. Adding pops of color in the distance to capture the visitor's gaze, pulling them to the end of the yard. These are the moments in a modern landscape that create beauty and stick with someone long after they've left.

Even if you feel that a modern design isn't right for you, I ask you to keep reading with an open mind. Even if the main elements don't fit what you've envisioned in your mind, you will still find inspiration and plant pointers that can apply to any design.

A cornerstone of this aesthetic starts with establishing a physical outline or silhouette. With this instance, the outline must be crisp and directional, many times in very straight lines. Frank Lloyd Wright's Fallingwater, the Barcelona Pavilion, and the Sydney Opera House are examples of modern architecture with their structural design making them global icons today. With razor sharp lines, use of metals and muted tones and the balance of man-made materials and natural elements create a beautiful balance.

As you take these concepts into a home setting, there are a few key items to keep in mind: materials, surrounding environment, existing

(ABOVE) Clean lines, repetition, and an intentional use of space result in a distinct boldness not found in other design styles.

(OPPOSITE) Large slabs of rectangular light concrete slabs visually held together by dark pebbles creates a stunning contrast. The addition of individual plants in pots and a small water garden, still in concrete, gives balance to the space by mixing hard and soft to create a still welcoming environment in a space created by hardscaping.

space, and the guardrails we discussed in Chapter 3. To maintain clear lines, a modern landscape design uses materials such as concrete, stone, metal, and milled wood. With an increasing focus on establishing a sense of place and supporting our neighbors, sourcing material that is intrinsic to the region has become increasingly popular, especially with lumber and stone. These materials deliver a sense of strength, intention, and boldness. They immediately set the tone for the entire space. And while that may seem like it will be cold and unnatural, the composition alongside natural plant material, soft tones of furniture, and inclusion of water features bring an orderly balance.

KELLY
The Naturalist

Dense and textural. Sustainability focused. Intentional wildness.

On the other extreme of Tommy's minimalism is Kelly's naturalistic approach to design and plant selection. In recent years, this concept of *New Naturalism* (the book written by this persona's namesake Kelly Norris) has become more and more mainstream as home gardeners are putting more of a focus on sustainability, native planting, and prairie-forward aesthetic. Kelly drives toward dense, ephemeral plantings that ooze personality, mystery, and wildness.

Kelly's natural landscape may be wild, but it's still intentional with structured looseness. The interplay of the mass planting has fabulously intertwined layers that not only showcase the best attributes of each plant species, but they thrive because each is selected because of Kelly's focus on place. This means that each plant is chosen because it is native to where it's being planted, or if it's not native, it has a similar cultural profile to plants that are from the area in which they're being planted. This is especially important as we continue to experience more drought, harsher conditions, and more fluctuations in temperature. Plants that are naturally adapted to a specific region have a leg up and require less maintenance once established.

I call Kelly The Naturalist, or even "The Collector," because this style of garden likely has the most unique plants of all. To create the diversity of color and texture, what this aesthetic yearns for requires distinction. Kelly doesn't rely on flowers, though they're a welcome bonus, but brings ornamental grasses and foliage-forward plants into the mix. This adds to the multi-season interest. There is always something to see in Kelly's garden.

The grass path running through this planting gives it a sense of place and provides order in an otherwise "wild" space.

Natural plantings in the Kelly style are prairie-like in their appearance, packed with plants (often native to the region), and organized with purposeful chaos.

One of the things that I love about this style is that it's a landscape that is gorgeous from afar, but it's meant to be viewed up close. This is a living landscape that begs for attention and admiration of its nuance and detail. It is vibrant and eclectic. It is pulls you through the landscape so that you can see all the judiciously selected cultivars at their peak.

Kelly's garden is all about the plants. But if hardscaping is integrated, it's likely local stone or other natural elements to accent the planting and not to outshine it. Though the garden may be planted in excess to start as it establishes, it may be edited over time to showcase the plants that have natural dominance. Some of Kelly's

(ABOVE) This Kelly-style garden has plants mingling together in a natural prairie-like fashion. The loose gravel selected for the walkway is a perfect fit.

(OPPOSITE) Though they may seem random and wild, the placement of each plant in a Kelly garden is made with intention. The naturalistic garden is a haven for pollinators and other wildlife.

plants may be sown directly as seeds, so that sense of mystery of what will thrive adds to the wild wonder of a naturalistic planting. This is an added element that makes visiting repeatedly such a gift. Not only does each season bring variety, but each year may show completely different heroes as plants arise from the seed bed and natural stressors such as drought, flood, heat, or cold cause plants to behave differently.

A final note about Kelly's design style is that collectors like to show off their wares. Of course, it's deeply personal, but many collectors and naturalistic designers like to teach and engage people with their landscapes. While they may not have as many structured hardscapes as you'd find in a Tommy- or Martha-style garden, a Kelly-style garden will likely have built a coffee nook or artist retreat into the gardens. What's more peaceful than a cup of coffee or painting the sunset in the middle of a buzzing meadow? Not a whole lot.

The Elements of Design

As we move into the elements of design and start putting to practice all that you've learned so far, keep these three personas in mind. As you were introduced to Martha, Tommy, and Kelly, you probably felt a connection to one of their gardens, or even elements from a couple. In the upcoming pages, I'll be sure to reference each of our friends and how the design element may apply to their style. Now's the time where we take your notes and worksheets from Chapters 2 and 3 and begin fleshing out a plan based on your personal aesthetic, now represented by our three personas.

I've broken up the main elements of design into ten themes. They may look familiar from Chapter 1, so we're not starting totally from scratch. Ten may seem like a lot, but I'll help break them down to useable ideas. And then in Chapter 5, I'll go one step further and take your persona, climate-driven considerations, and these design themes and pull them into plant palettes that you can use. See, I promised I'd make it easy on you! Ready? Let's go!

Including neutrals like this fuzzy silver-leafed Iceberg Alley sageleaf willow pairs well with plants around it that change color throughout the season and also brightens up the landscape in a time of year where others aren't yet at peak.

Color

To discuss the use of color in garden design, we're going to take a trip back to elementary school. Remember ROYGBV? Red, orange, yellow, green, blue, and violet. The color wheel that brightened our childhood is back, and now it's going to lead us to a more beautiful yard. It's a simplistic but easy tool that can help you nail the all-important color aspect of your design. There are a couple of things to consider before we get into some color theory.

One is to keep in mind neutral colors that will balance out the others that brighten up the landscape. In standard color theory, you'll see gray, brown, and black listed, but there aren't many plants with those as primary colors. Some go-to plants with silver foliage include Silver Mound artemisia (*Artemisia schmidtiana* 'Silver Mound'), Lamb's Ear (*Stachys byzantine*), Dusty Miller (*Senecio cineraria*), and Iceberg Alley sageleaf willow (*Salix candida* 'Jefberg'). With a relatively small plant palette with those neutral colors, a bonus is that green also can serve as neutral in the landscape too. That opens a huge array of green-leaf plants, both evergreen and deciduous (plants that lose their leaves in winter).

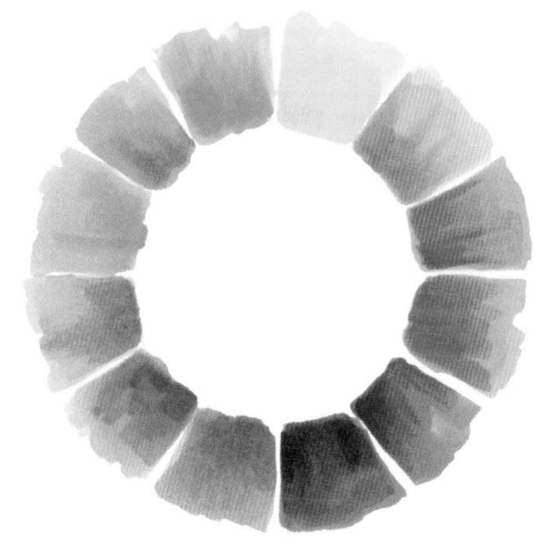

The color wheel can be used to select color themes for your garden.

At the time this photo was taken, the monochromatic color palette of this large naturalistic planting falls in the pink to lavender range, though throughout the season, other colors come into play as other plants come into bloom.

A second thing to keep in mind is the seasonality of color. A plant that blooms white in summer may be pink or red in fall (think panicle hydrangeas), so make sure that you keep the plant's full color cycle in mind as you work your way around the color wheel. With that, let's look at a few key theories to get you started.

MONOCHROMATIC. This straightforward design is all about choosing a color you love and plastering it all over the garden. If you love pink, let's plan a pink garden for you! If you love blue, let's sing the blues all over your backyard. While the monochromatic color can make a big statement, I like to add some variety so that the design doesn't get stale. Add different shades of your choice color or different plant species with a unique leaf color or shape. This will keep that impact of your favorite color while adding a bit more texture and variation.

The bold, complementary colors of this garden add excitement to the landscape.

A combination of monochromatic and analogous color schemes, this mixture of Grape Lollipop, Cotton Candy, and Bubblegum Pink phlox (*Phlox paniculata*) makes you say "wow," and the variation in color within the pink-purple scale keeps things interesting.

ANALOGOUS. Taking one step around the color wheel, analogous combinations take plants with leaf and/or flower colors that are next to each other on the color wheel and mix them in the landscape. This means red or orange and yellow or green and blue are fabulous options. Most of the time, this also keeps the warm and cool colors together, which affects the mood and feeling of the landscape. Cool colors create a calm, relaxing environment where warm colors can add energy and action to the garden.

COMPLEMENTARY. Taking a bigger leap around the wheel, complementary colors are those that are across from each other: red and green, violet and yellow, and blue and orange. This really makes the garden pop and makes you look. This is a fun one to play with seasonality. Certain times of year when plants aren't in flower, they may be analogous with green foliage and a blue flower next door (maybe Russian sage or delphinium), but when the flowers emerge orange (maybe a lantana or red hot poker), it adds the drama of becoming a complementary scheme. When those colors collide, it's quite the show.

TRIAD. To add a little more complexity—and a lot more drama—to your design, let's talk about using three of the major colors on the color wheel. To do this, we connect those that aren't already neighbors: red, yellow, and blue are one triad and violet, orange, and green form the other triad. Planting these in one bed gives that extra bit of dimension that, in my opinion, makes the design feel more organic and realistic than the plant-mulch-plant-mulch phenomenon that we see in so many commercial installations. The more diversity and complexity that we add, with structure and intention of course, the more lush and more organic the garden will feel.

What Would Martha, Tommy, and Kelly Do?

Now that we've got the basics, it's time to start thinking about how you'll put the color theory to work in your garden. So, let's check back with our friends Martha, Tommy, and Kelly and see what they'd do.

Martha's a bit of a wild card here. Her classic approach is probably most connected with the monochromatic and analogous schemes but may venture into complementary colors as she gets more comfortable with digging in the dirt. Remember that she's about style and substance without spending hours on the work, so she's going for what looks great and might be a bit quicker to assemble.

Tommy is really focused on the monochromatic look. That modern approach is especially in tune with the neutral colors, so ornamental grasses that have the brown plumes are especially in vogue. Because drastic use of color is not typical in minimalistic design, focus on one solid color is most likely.

Kelly is likely to use a combination of these approaches, especially as seasonal displays. Because of the diversity of his plant palette, he can do so much more with color. The selection of more native plants will add a fantastic base of neutral colors, and the pops of color from his structural shrubs and interwoven perennials, annuals, and grasses will give seasonal touches with each turn of the color wheel.

This Martha style garden has many vivid colors. Maybe you like it, or maybe you don't. The use of color in your own backyard is a personal—and important—decision.

Texture

I know I overuse this word when I talk about gardens and design, but it's just so important. Texture adds depth and dimension to the landscape to keep it interesting. It takes a garden from being good to great. Your wardrobe would be boring if it was all the same, right? You need your leggings, jeans, T-shirts, date night outfits, and formalwear. And don't forget the accessories to top off the look. Same with the garden.

Building texture into your outdoor space is a way to engage the senses, and that's what makes it special and memorable. Beyond observing beauty and variation of color and shape with sight, choosing plants with fuzzy leaves or flowers, for example, is a great way to add texture to the landscape while engaging the sense of touch. Gardens should be interactive, so if you can encourage people to participate simply by choosing the right plant, you've earned some bonus points. Some of my favorites include the velvety flowers of Mexican bush sage (*Salvia leucantha*), the late-season plumes of fountain grass (*Pennisetum*), the fuzzy leaves of mullein (*Verbascum thapsus*), the poufy blooms of the smoke tree (*Cotinus coggygria*), and the fine-textured foliage of yarrow (*Achillea millefolium*).

There are a number of ways to create a more textured and layered landscape. As you begin to select plants that fit your aesthetic and will thrive in your region in Chapter 5, keep these in mind so that your garden becomes the showstopper you've set out to create.

Plants with different foliage and flower forms add texture to the garden, along with the materials used for the hardscaping and the home itself. Here, Japanese forest grass (*Hakonechloa*) creates a soft edge along a front walk.

The possibilities are endless when it comes to the ability of flowers to add a textural element to the garden. The structure and shape of each bloom provides something different.

As light passes through the leaf of the canna lily (*Canna* × *generalis*), you can see the amazing painted lines that run through, giving great depth to the garden without the use of one singular flower.

FLOWERS. Beyond color, the flower heads themselves can add drama and delight. Varying size and shape of the blooms, petals, and variegation all matter. In the spring garden, the smooth upright petals of tulips (*Tulipia* spp.) underplanted with the star-shaped spikes of pink hyacinth (*Hyacinth orientalis*) and blue cones of muscari (*Muscari armeniacum*) not only bring a triad of color, but the three different shapes and sizes of the blooms is incredibly interesting to see and draws you in to look closer. While these spring bulbs' blooms are fleeting, you can try a texture-filled combination in the summer garden with the flat yellow petals of black-eyed Susans (*Rudbekia hirta*), blue-purple spikes of catmint (*Nepeta* spp.), and white cones of panicle hydrangeas (*Hydrangea paniculata*). What a sight! The different shape of each petal and the form and size of the plants all make that summer planting multi-dimensional and full of character. This is what adds to the wow factor.

FOLIAGE. Flowers are amazing, but the underrated stars of the garden are leaves. There are so many exceptional shapes, colors, and patterns that make foliage the center of attention. This is especially important in shade gardens where fewer showy flowering plants thrive. Just because there aren't flowers doesn't mean it can't be a focal point, and even in sunny, flower-filled gardens, interesting leaves can steal the show from a bloom any day. I especially love to mix different-shaped leaves to create dimension. Finely shaped foliage can be like little daggers emerging from the garden bed. Adam's needle (*Yucca filamentosa*), the foliage of Siberian iris (*Iris siberica*) after the flowers fade, and Hakone grass (*Hakonechloa macra*) are some of my favorites. On the flip side, plants with broad leaves can really fill some space and make a name for themselves. Some of my favorite showoffs are coral bells (*Heuchera* hybrids), umbrella plant (*Darmera peltate*), elephant ears (*Colocasia esculenta*), canna (*Canna* spp.), and hostas (*Hosta* spp.). Pairing the thin leaves with the broad leaves gives variation, surprise, and complexity that makes your garden stand out against a more standard plant-mulch-plant-mulch garden design.

The seed head of northern sea oats grass glows in the golden hour light of fall. It's impossible to ignore their beauty in the late-season landscape.

SEEDS. I'll start talking about seeds with a caveat. Some flowers go to seed and then spread all over the place and become invasive. We talked about invasive plants in Chapter 2, so you'll definitely want to avoid anything that's going to take over the garden, but there are so many plants and especially ornamental grasses that form fabulous seed heads that add seasonal texture to the landscape. Many of these develop later in the season and are a perfect way to keep your winter garden interesting in climates where many plants lose their leaves. An exceptional standout when it comes to late-season seeds are the wispy remains of a clematis (*Clematis* spp.) bloom that turn into whirling feathers extending from the base of where the flower once was. Not only does this extend the beauty of the vine, but it also adds different textures in different seasons with flat petals while in flower to feathery, wind-blown puffs as the growing season progresses. Other favorites that add texture with seeds or seed heads include seven-son flower (*Heptacodium miconioides*), coneflower (*Echinacea* spp.), poppy (*Papaver* spp.), sea holly (*Eryngium* spp.), and a whole mix of ornamental grasses, such northern sea oats (*Chasmanthium latifolium*), fountain grass (*Pennisetum* spp.), pampas grass (*Cortaderia selloana*), and maiden grass (*Miscanthus* spp.).

Adding plants that create noninvasive seed heads is one of my favorite ways to extend the seasons of the garden. Especially in cooler climates like mine, it's like the Band-Aid between the lushness of summer and early bulb-driven flowers of spring.

HARDSCAPE. As you plan out your landscaping projects, plants aren't the only way to add texture to the garden. Thinking about the materials you'll use to create structure can make a difference in the feeling of your space. The rough texture of brick will give you a different feel than a smooth poured concrete patio, as will a mulch path versus a pea gravel path. Thinking back to your overall design goals—as well as how you'll use the space—will really drive these decisions, but now you can also add the layer of how the texture pairs with that vision. Not to mention the planting plan you're putting around it. If you're going with a wilder planting, the unevenness of natural materials can be a great pairing. If you're opting for a super modern design, you probably wouldn't include rustic reclaimed wood along your planters. All the pieces come together to tell your story, and the complementary or intentionally disparate textures of the living plant material and tactile hardscaping fill your garden with dimension and personality.

The hardscaping in your garden includes the pathways, retaining walls, decks, porches, and patios. The materials you use should complement your design style and your house.

What Would Martha, Tommy, and Kelly Do?

Let's check back with our friends Martha, Tommy, and Kelly on texture. This is a fun one that can show off their personalities easily.

Let's start with **Kelly**, whose naturalistic approach is all about texture. The overlapping planting design beseeches the constant ebb and flow of an evolving landscape. As one season wanes, another is just taking off. Summer's flowers and combination of leaf colors, shapes, and sizes churn into fall's ornamental grasses making their debut before hardening off to give architectural prominence in winter. Each one of these textural moments are celebrated in Kelly's design.

One step removed, **Martha** wouldn't be as bold as Kelly but would want to mix these techniques into a more structured space. With less plant material, the focus is on making more prominent choices with contrasting leaf shapes, colorful patterns, and more intentional plumes of feathery grass texture. Martha would also be very specific about her use of hardscape to complement her plantings; there's less contrast here in an effort to have a classically beautiful look. Think slate pavers along a colorful, lush pathway and less fieldstone slightly covered by multiple plants (intentionally) spilling over.

Tommy is going to have a more rigid approach when it comes to texture. While it's important to provide some contrast from the clean lines of this style, texture is used with constraint. That slight variation keeps the space from being boring, but you don't want to go overboard or it will feel disjointed. Tommy would use sharp, clean edges in hardscaping, structural plants such as Blackhawks big bluestem (*Andropogon gerardii*) and Straight & Narrow® Japanese holly (*Ilex crenata*) to bring color and variation in natural texture without getting too delicate or frothy.

Foliage and flowers bring so many different textures and forms to the landscape. Here, spiky foliage combines with frothy blooms and varied foliage colors to make a stunning front yard.

Seasonality

Designing for the seasons all goes back to Chapter 3 when we talked about how you're going to use your space. If you're designing for a summer home, that's totally different than if you're living in the landscape year-round. So as always, think back to the motivation behind these projects and then pick out the advice that's most relevant to you. For most of my projects, I'm looking at building a four-season garden. Every day of the year should be inspiring and beautiful, and not brushed aside because the deciduous plants are bare. There are way too many cool plants with off-season interest to have any bland days.

Now, my natural perspective is sort of skewed here because I live in a cold climate with a short growing season, so building a landscape with fabulous fall, winter, and spring beauty is more challenging but equally important as those of you who live in a more subtropical climate such as Georgia, the Carolinas, the Florida peninsula, the Azores, or the Po Valley in northern Italy. While you can grow plants year-round, there are still elements of seasonal interest that break the cycle of a stagnant outdoor space.

To work through this conversation about seasonality in the garden, I'm going to break it down by the four main seasons and give ideas on how to create something uniquely special for each time of year. Keep in mind that this can vary a bit based on where you live, so as you dive into plant selection in Chapter 5, I'll be sure to give more options that fit your specific climate. But this will start to give you a broad strokes approach to get the ball rolling.

WINTER. I like to start in the least traditional month you think of for outdoor gardening because why not kick this off with a challenge,

A winter garden in California is much different than my experience in Minnesota. But that doesn't stop us from having fun up here in the frozen tundra!

Even in winter, a well-designed landscape looks lovely when you've selected a mixture of plants that are suited to your region.

Now, I'm not one to judge because I choose to live in a place with impossibly cold winters, but seeing a blooming camellia (*Camellia* spp.) in January would sure make me feel pretty darn good. The fire-red stem of Neon Burst dogwood (*Cornus alba* 'ByBoughen') sure does reflect well against the bright white of newly fallen snow.

right? If we can make a garden beautiful in winter, we can make it beautiful any time. Again, the caveat being that if you live in a hot tropical climate, this may not be the case, but stick with me. To me, winter gardening is all about creating surprising moments of delight. In a time when you think of dreary and drab colors and a muted space that you avoid, I try to create moments that pull you back into the garden, even if there's a foot of snow outside. The red stems of a red-twig dogwood (*Cornus* spp.), hoarfrost-covered hydrangea (*Hydrangea* spp.) blooms glistening in the soft morning light, and the bright red berries of winterberry (*Ilex verticillata*) create such an unexpected glimmer of hope for the growing season to come. It lights a fire that may have diminished during the dark doldrums of winter. Early blooming bulbs such as snowdrops (*Galanthus* spp.), Lenten rose (*Helleborus* spp.), and crocus (*Crocus* spp.) can peek their way through snow-covered lawns for the earliest of blooms, coupled with color from witch hazel's (*Hamamelis* spp.) bright, crinkle paper blooms, winter heath's (*Erica carnea*) protrusion of pink; or bloodroot's (*Sanguinaria* spp.) cuplike flowers that emerge low to the ground before the trees begin to bud.

In subtropic or tropic regions where you rarely, if ever, have a frost, you can really live it up by planting cold-season vegetables, such as lettuce, onions, English peas, or carrots, or by celebrating winter-blooming shrubs such as anise tree (*Illicium* spp.), fringe flower (*Loropetalum chinense*), camellias (*Camellia* spp.), and winter jasmine (*Jasminum nudiflorum*). We cold-climate gardeners are envious of your ability to eat fresh from the garden in January, so take full advantage and be sure to post on Instagram so we can live vicariously through you as we hunker down in parkas! In the more temperate or warm climates, winter is a great time of year to plan for and plant your garden for the upcoming spring and summer. Since the weather is much less harsh than your hot summers, getting plants in the ground now gives them a fighting chance to establish their root systems to pull up the necessary water and nutrients in the blazing heat of summer. Once you finish that holiday shopping, it's time to treat yourself with some plants for the garden! Just be sure to bear in mind what your other seasons' weather will bring so you don't fry anything you spent your hard-earned money on in the coming months.

SPRING. As the great American gardener and author Ruth Stout once said, "I love spring anywhere, but if I could choose, I would always greet it in a garden." This time of emerging into a new season of warmth and sunshine breathes fresh life into us as the ground warms up and delivers flowers, foliage, and hope. Think about your experience as the sloshy rain and melting snow gives way to that first beautiful spring day. You feel rejuvenated. And the garden feels the same. You get to see how your landscape fared over the winter months and, if there are any losses, what opportunity you have to try something new. I know I've beaten this drum a hundred times, but plants are living things and sometimes don't make it. So instead of getting bummed, look at it as an opportunity for a new plant to take its place!

Since spring gives us this feeling of rebirth, I like to kick things off with a bang in cooler climates. Combining bulbs, perennials, and shrubs that like to show off in spring with successional flowers or leaves emerging fills up the garden quickly and accelerates the transition from winter bones to a lush landscape. If you layer

Spring-flowering trees are one of the first harbingers of spring in the garden. These crabapples stand out against the black siding of this modern home.

bulbs based on their planting depth, you can have those amazing winter blooms I mentioned before, and as they start to fade, your spring blooms—daffodils (*Narcissus* spp.), tulips (*Tulipa* spp.), Siberian squill (*Scilla siberica*), and iris (*Iris* spp.)—can take over the show. So you're not completely reliant on bulbs—in case some pesky squirrels dig some up for a winter snack—other favorite spring bloomers in cool climates are shade-loving bleeding hearts (*Dicentra spectabilis*), carpet-like creeping phlox (*Phlox subulate*), the unfurling of fiddleheads on ostrich ferns (*Matteuccia struthiopteris*), peonies (*Paeonia* spp.), alpine asters (*Aster alpinus*), ninebark (*Physocarpus opulifolius*), deciduous azaleas (*Rhododendron* spp.), and Saskatoon serviceberry (*Amelanchier alnifolia*). The succession of these blooms and leaves may depend on your climate, so you'll want to do a little digging on when they start to unfurl in your area, but you can time it so that you've got something new putting on a show in the garden every week of spring.

Even in warm climates where you have more evergreen plants and can grow vegetables year-round, the spring garden still brings additional flashes of color and the opportunity for a lush landscape as evening temperatures rise and the risk of a frost diminishes. Just like the cool climates, azaleas are one of the most well-known starters to a spring landscape in the southern United States due to The Masters Golf Tournament. I've had the great honor of attending The Masters with their horticultural consultant, and the precision they have in getting those azaleas to be in perfect bloom on time in April is incredible. Because you're starting off with a fuller landscape than those of us with more deciduous gardens in cold climates, I like to focus on the pops of seasonal color and texture to make spring special. Early spring is a great time to get annuals in the ground, in baskets, or in your pots so they can start to put on some growth before the heat of summer settles in.

Since these are planted annually, it gives you the chance to create new themes every year. Other perennials and shrubs that I love for spring in a warm climate are the drought-tolerant yarrow (*Achillea millefolium*), doublefile viburnum (*Viburnum plicatum*), witch alder (*Fothergilla* spp.), pincushion (*Scabiosa caucasica*), and redbud (*Cercis canadensis*).

SUMMER. The height of the luscious gardening season is ushered in during the summer months; it is the grand crescendo of the annual garden display. Designing a summer garden is all about celebration of what you love most. That could be color or texture, it could be a singular kind of plant, or it may just be creating the most beautiful yard to host family and friends while the weather cooperates. Creating these moments is such a fun endeavor and allows you to show off some personality.

Summer is the time to enjoy and maintain the garden. It's a really tough time to plant due to higher temperatures, so unless you've got a special reason to plant, you can put that shovel away and enjoy yourself. For that reason, think back to Chapter 2 and how you intend to use your outdoor space and plan to plant for summer either in spring or fall. Bear in mind the summer weather conditions in your region when you're choosing plants. Do you have regular rainfall that can temper the high temperatures? Or are you in a more arid or desertlike climate? Do you have big fluctuations in weather or is the weather pretty consistent? All these factors should come into play because the summer months can be some of the most stressful on your plants, so you'll want to be sure they can take it.

No matter your climate or ultimate design scheme, you can add lots of variation in your summer garden. Like the spring-blooming azaleas at The Masters, if we had to name summer's classic bloom, it'd probably be the hydrangea.

Still one of the most popular shrubs in the world, these blooms fill millions of gardens with characteristic summer beauty. There are a ton of species of hydrangea, but three reign supreme in summer: bigleaf hydrangea (*Hydrangea macrophylla*), panicle hydrangea (*Hydrangea paniculata*), and smooth hydrangea (*Hydrangea arborescens*). You can plant these bad boys as a focal point, in swaths of color, or in pots to brighten up a patio. The list of summer-blooming shrubs and perennials could fill the rest of this book, so I won't list them all. But in Chapter 5, I'll share lots more ideas on how to fill up the summer garden with more than just hydrangea.

The last thing to mention about summer gardening is something I mention over and over in this book. When possible, find plants that extend beyond one season. Yes, getting some amazing summer color or mass from a plant is fabulous, but if you can also get some fall interest or winter texture, that's a plant that's earning its place in the landscape. Extending seasons and getting more bang for your buck is the way to go in my mind. As you're choosing recipes in the coming pages, keep that in mind. If summer color is your focus, fantastic, but what else does each plant give to you and your landscape?

The lush, tropical summer vibes of this garden pot help create the perfect place to entertain family and friends.

(NEXT PAGE) Don't get tricked into thinking summer color is all there is. Be sure to include as many plants with four-seasons of interest as possible. When these summer annuals and perennials fade, the evergreens and shrubs will need to step in.

FALL. It's hard to find a time where I don't love being in a garden, but fall is one of those moments where I just fall deeper in love. The lushness of summer is amazing, but as temperatures cool down, I find that fall is the season where you can really enjoy sitting in your creation. It's still sumptuous after the growing season's hard work, but the space just becomes more livable. Not only that, but you start to see so much transformation in a short amount of time. Leaves begin to change, flower colors adapt to the cooler evenings, ornamental grasses arise from the ground to take center stage. It can just be so darn beautiful and full.

Designing for a fall garden can be a test of patience, as this is the furthest from when the garden starts to emerge in late winter and spring. But gardens can bring such a sense of pride and ownership that the resiliency of waiting for the garden's big hurrah before the winter settles in can be really special. As you're laying out your planting plan, consider what you want to be the showpieces of your fall garden and how much space they'll take as they establish.

Break the cycle of orange, red, and yellow in fall by adding cool color flowers such as Sapphire Surf bluebeard, which blooms late in the season. The pops of blue flowers create unexpected moments in the fall garden and raise you above the level of pedestrian gardening.

If you're planning late summer- or fall-blooming bulbs such as dahlia (*Dahlia* spp.), ivy-leaved cyclamen (*Cyclamen hederifolium*), or saffron crocus (*Crocus sativus*), they can be underplanted to pop up in the garden as other plants begin to fade or to give some late season color under tree canopies. These bulbs don't take up much space, especially outside of their growing season, so the underplanting technique is a great way to keep the garden full and not have gaps for spring and summer.

Planting shrubs and trees for fall will take up year-round space, so keep that in mind—and not just how much space they take up today, but in the future. Check the plant tag for the mature size and plan accordingly. I've had so many conversations with home gardeners about pruning back their shrubs because they got too big. If you plant for mature size, you'll save yourself a lot of headaches in the future. Shrubs such as panicle or oakleaf hydrangeas (*Hydrangea paniculata* and *Hydrangea quercifolia*, respectively), St. John's Wort (*Hypericum inodorum*), chokeberry (*Aronia arbutifolia*), and cutleaf staghorn sumac (*Rhus typhina*) bring color and texture to the garden in other seasons, but really show off in fall.

In between the mass of shrubs or trees and bulbs, you've got a huge number of perennials and ornamental grasses that are undeniably stunning in fall. Sky blue asters (*Symphyotrichum oolentangiense*), hardy mums (*Chrysanthemum* spp.), sneezeweed (*Helenium autumnale*), stonecrop (*Sedum* spp.), and pink muhly grass (*Muhlenbergia capillaris*) are some of my favorites. Each of these may get cut back in fall or late winter, leaving a gap in the early part of the growing season, so you'll want to plant some spring-blooming bulbs or perennials to fill the space if you're like Kelly and prefer a more densely filled garden.

What would Martha, Tommy, and Kelly do?

I covered a lot of ground talking about planting for four seasons, but this design element impacts so many others, so it deserves the attention. Unless you determined that you're only planning for a one-season garden at a vacation home, understanding how the seasons work together, how the plants transition, and how to plan your space needs to be top of mind. If we revisit the design minds of Tommy, Martha, and Kelly, this is one of the design elements where they'll have more alignment than disparity. In most cases, all design styles will incorporate elements of multi-season interest. Each may incorporate the same type of plant, but in slightly different ways.

Tommy may plant masses of bulbs with straight edges to achieve a structured mass of spring color. Looking at seasonal ornamental grasses in fall, Tommy would choose varieties with more upright growth habit, such as the spear-shaped New Zealand flax (*Phormium tenax*).

Martha may use pockets of bulbs mixed in with her shrubs to add splotches of color like polka dots. Martha would look for a reliable, hard-working, low-input grass, such as world-renowned Karl Foerster feather reed grass (*Calamagrostis x acutiflora*) to add texture to her fall garden.

Kelly may use bulbs more sporadically to give a free-flowing inclusion of these blooms that would echo a Pollock painting. Kelly's use of ornamental grasses in fall would focus on those that adds hazy texture, such as purple lovegrass (*Eragrostis spectabilis*).

Ornamental grasses and perennials with colorful fall foliage are a hallmark of Kelly-style designs that foster four-season interest.

Function

I know you already spent some time thinking about how your outdoor space needs to function: entertaining, holding a hillside in place, collecting rainwater, etc. Now we get to actually bring plants into the mix, move from the why and dig into the how. The thought of function in and of itself isn't the sexiest part of design, but the doors that it opens really are exciting. You can have fashion and function, and in many cases in the living landscape, they're both necessary. If you found that you have challenging soil or light conditions in Chapter 2, choosing plants for function is step number one. That doesn't mean it won't be beautiful, but we've got to solve the ecological challenges first.

Plants are powerful. They have adapted to create sustainable life in sometimes the harshest of conditions and are still here today. We can—and should—take cues from them on how to best use them in the landscape, especially if you're fighting against a less-than-ideal situation to create a home landscape. Plant selection is about the soil you're planting in, water availability, anticipating climate change, and also using structure to create moments in your outdoor space. It's a mutually beneficial, symbiotic relationship between plants, the ecosystem of your yard, and the aesthetic value they provide.

When I approach design as it relates to function, I start with the unavoidable issues first and use that as the foundation. If you have heavy clay soil, that will affect your plant selection. If you have a spot in your yard that holds water through the spring months, we have to deal with that. If you live in an arid climate that sees little to no rain, we won't be planting hydrangeas. Check back to your notes from Chapter 2 and figure out what challenges your landscape offers, and then make a plan. These challenges don't have to stop you in your tracks; I'll help you find the solutions.

This naturalistic planting and retaining wall help stabilize a slope while providing nectar for pollinators, two very important functions.

This patio-adjacent garden is filled primarily with plants native to the region. It was planted in unamended soil. The density of the planting means there is little room for weeds.

SOIL. There are a few ways to approach the functionality of planting with soil. The first is simply choosing plants that do well in the existing soil your site offers. Remember your brunch date from Chapter 2 where you determined what kind of soil you have? Time to dig those notes back out and refresh what types of plants do well in whatever mix you've got. Remember that in Chapter 5 I'll give some more specific recipes, but if you can take what you learned before and use it to narrow your focus on plant material, that'll make your life a lot easier and less frustrating if plants don't work out in the future. For example, you wouldn't plant lavender in clay soil because it retains too much water and will cause the roots to rot. It might look okay at first, but once you get some rain, you'll start to see the plant go downhill. Another option—especially if you have a plant that you love and need to have in your garden, but it doesn't do well with the soil you already have—is to amend the soil before planting. With the lavender example, you could amend the clay soil with peat moss to increase the drainage and keep that baby alive. Amending the soil is also important if you have more alkaline soil with a high pH and you want blueberries or azaleas, which prefer acidic soils with low pH. Adding a soil acidifier at planting and in the subsequent growing seasons can help lower the pH and make those plants thrive. Sometimes this is just too much work if you've got a busy schedule, but know that if your soil isn't ideal, you can help it along to fit the plants you want in the garden.

Having healthy soil is really important for the long-term outputs of the landscape. Not only does the soil mix matter, but having nutrients in the ground is what will keep those plants thriving for years to come. A natural wood chip mulch—avoid the colored mulch, if possible—will decompose over time and add nutrients to the soil. And those pesky leaves that cover your lawn in fall? Instead of bagging them and sending them off, compost them and use them to add nutrients to your soil at home. Non-waxy leaves such as maple, birch, crabapple, and beech trees are especially quick to break down. Run them over with the lawnmower to get them chopped up and pile them in a corner of your yard to start breaking down. Adding some grass clippings, green food scraps, or eggshells will infuse nitrogen to the mix, which will speed up the composting process. Turn the pile every week or so and make sure that it stays moist, kind of like a wrung-out sponge, and depending on your climate, your leaf pile will decompose to soil-like crumbly material that can be spread on top of your garden and infuse tons of great nutrients into the soil. If your design style matches Kelly, you may not use wood chip mulch to cover open space in the garden, but instead use groundcovers and low grasses to fill the gaps. As this material gets cut back, it continues to act as a weed suppressant like all mulch and will decompose and add nutrients to the soil below.

WATER. An escalating issue around the globe, water usage is rightfully in the spotlight and many people are planning garden spaces to minimize how much water is needed for them to thrive. This can be done through several tactics, including plant selection, creating water retention systems, and switching to drip irrigation. Whether you're in an area that has water issues or not, chances are you will see the need for drought-resistant design coming soon. Let's stay ahead of the curve and make smart choices now!

Choosing drought-tolerant plants is becoming easier each year as plant breeders introduce newer and better genetics that allow this type of plant to still be beautiful. Fashion and function. California poppy (*Eschscholzia californica*), scarlet sage (*Salvia splendens*), threadleaf coreopsis (*Coreopsis verticillata*), columbine (*Aquilegia* spp.), bougainvillea (*Bougainvillea* spp.), and distylium (*Distylium* spp.) are a small selection of some of my favorites. Check out any list of plants for a rock garden and you should be in good shape, assuming they're a right fit for your climate.

Another term you may have come across if you're looking for a low water input garden is xeriscaping. This is a practice that's aimed at conserving water usage by pairing plants with similar water needs or maximizing the use of drought-tolerant plants. Native plants are already adapted to your site and will likely need less water than some nonnative plants, so if you pair them all together, you're creating an ecosystem that will need little, if any, supplemental water. Another element of xeriscaping is to reduce the amount of turf grass used for your lawn. Grass can be a water hog, especially in times of drought, so reducing that turf footprint and replacing it with native plants has become a big trend to be more sustainable. If you do need some supplemental water in your garden beds, setting up a drip irrigation system can greatly reduce the amount of water you use since it applies the water right to the base of the plants in need, rather than scattering it around like a hose nozzle or a sprinkler. Drip irrigation systems can

This drought-tolerant street-side planting of grasses, upright junipers, lavender, and sedum provides plenty of texture and interest against the blank backdrop of the wall. This is a great example of a Tommy-style design: simple repetition with clean lines.

be DIY and remain pretty inexpensive, and they can really have a major impact on your water bill and the resources needed to keep your landscape looking picturesque.

If you're on the other end of the spectrum and you have seasons where you experience a lot of water, there are some things you can do to capitalize on those moments and still have a focus on sustainability, even in times of excess. Rain gardens have become increasingly popular, especially as the concrete jungles of our cities continue expansion. Water can't permeate the concrete and tar, so it runs off and picks up chemicals and other pollutants before running back into the soil and our water supply. Rain gardens are planting spaces built into a depression where a lot of runoff may occur. Typically using native plant species for your region, the planting not only serves as a pool for that excess water to fill, but the plants filter the pollution out as the water soaks back into the earth. Pretty darn cool, huh? If you don't have an area with a lot of runoff, but you've got areas in your yard that retain a lot of moisture in certain times of year, you can choose plants that like "wet feet," or don't mind having their roots sitting in excess moisture. The plant sucks up that excess water versus creating pools in your yard. Flip forward a few pages to the case study of my house where you'll see that I have this exact situation in my backyard. As snow melts in spring, the primary focal point becomes a water-logged pool and so I've planted Fiber Optics buttonbush (*Cephalantus occidentalis*), Firedance dogwood (*Cornus sericea*), and northern blue flag iris (*Iris versicolor*) that not only soak up the spring water, but also give some great color to the early season garden.

UTILITY. Adapting for soil and water are key elements to the function of design, but there are other utilitarian uses for plants (that can also be beautiful). My theme of function and fashion continues; they don't need to be mutually exclusive, or life would be boring. Plants are problem solvers. Using the right plant in the right place can make your problems disappear. Just like buttonbush soaks up spring water in wet spots of the yard, other plants can be used to create screens between properties, hold together a slippery hillside, and create shade on the hot edge of your house.

Now look, I love my neighbors. We got so lucky that both families adjacent to our new house are amazing and fun and we've become friends. But not everyone is so lucky, and you might want to create a little bit of privacy. Establishing a hedge doesn't have to be a middle finger to them. It can be a beautiful border between properties to shield a pool or hot tub, keep your dog from barking at activity next door, or build a beautiful focal point with a mass of elevated color. I guess it could be a bit of a middle finger, but you can soften the blow by using one of these excuses. You can always go the classic arborvitae (*Thuja* spp.) or privet (*Ligustrum* spp.) hedge route (if privet isn't invasive in your region). Or get a little more creative and use a midsize crape myrtle such as Lunar Magic (*Lagerstroemia* 'Baillagone'), panicle hydrangea (*Hydrangea paniculata*), serviceberry (*Amelanchier alnifolia*), Japanese holly (*Ilex crenata*), or lilac (*Syringa* spp.).

Since I do love my neighbors, I'm not going to put a screening hedge along our property line, but it is a massive downslope, so I want to plant the hillside to prevent runoff and keep everything in place. While the turf grass does an okay job, I want to put shrubs in the ground to establish deeper roots that will act like glue to keep it all together. The plants also will soften the hardscaping stairs that we're building into the hill to give it a more natural look, evening out the entire appearance of the rough hill. When planning a sloped garden,

The flowers on Fiber Optics® buttonbush are an added bonus to the functional benefits of the plant. Not only are they fun to look at, but they're fabulous for pollinators, and as they dry into seed heads, they're waterfowl snacks.

I like to use a mix of shrubs and perennials so the root systems reach differing depths to hold the soil in place. Some of my favorites for a hillside garden include Jade Parade sand cherry (*Prunus pumila* 'UCONNPP002'), shrub roses (*Rosa* spp.), bugleweed (*Ajuga* spp.), periwinkle (*Vinca minor*), snowberry (*Symphoricarpos* spp.), shrubby cinquefoil (*Potentilla fruticosa*), and little bluestem grass (*Schizachyrium scoparium*).

One last utilitarian idea to give you a break from summer sun and help your pocketbook is planting large shrubs and trees to give shade to your yard. You can create spaces for moments of relaxation away from the summer heat or you can save on your electrical bill by reducing the direct impact of the sun's rays through your windows. You're reducing your net carbon footprint by planting trees and seeing some tangible benefit to your lifestyle. Win, win, win. I love talking to people about planting shade trees, and if you've got space, I always try to mix them into planting design. There are compact varieties being introduced fairly regularly to allow shade trees a place in the suburban or urban home garden, but if you've got a little extra land and can plant a gorgeous noble tree such as an elm (*Ulmus* spp.), oak (*Quercus* spp.), hickory (*Carya* spp.), beech (*Fagus* spp.), maple (*Acer* spp.), or bald cypress (*Taxodium* spp.), please do so. You may not live to see it in its full glory, but your kids and grandkids will thank you.

This classic Martha gardener has created a wonderful sense of privacy by surrounding their property with plantings of evergreens and hedges. The result is a veritable private oasis.

Negative space, whether it's an open lawn, an empty bed, or a vacant deck, opens views and provides "breathing room."

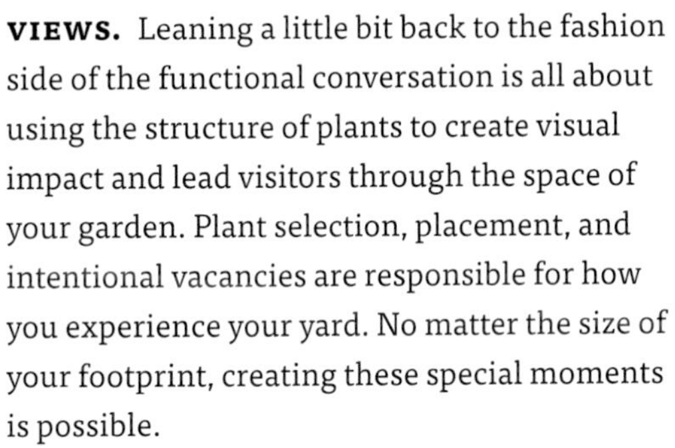

VIEWS. Leaning a little bit back to the fashion side of the functional conversation is all about using the structure of plants to create visual impact and lead visitors through the space of your garden. Plant selection, placement, and intentional vacancies are responsible for how you experience your yard. No matter the size of your footprint, creating these special moments is possible.

When designing a garden, I always find ways to incorporate negative space, or the areas between the plantings that provide contrast, light, and a visual break. To do this, you could include a piece of circular garden art that opens to the sky beyond, allowing light into the garden and a break from the color and texture of the plant material. You could design curved garden beds that open to a turf area or hardscaping with a patio set, the break from the garden serving as contrasting negative space to the fullness of the garden. By bringing these clean and idle spaces to a landscape, it gives the brain and eyes a break and provides a resting place so that the rest of the garden may be enjoyed that much more.

In line with negative space is the focus on using light in the garden. Whether man-made or natural, some of the most special moments in the garden are defined by the light. You know that golden hour selfie that everyone loves to post on social media? Take away the cell phone and imagine the basking glow of sunset radiating behind the floral display you've created in your yard. It's nothing short of magical. Think back again to Chapters 2 and 3 when you learned about the light in your space and when you'll likely be in the garden. Where is the light coming from at different parts of the day? When do you want to enjoy it the most? Knowing that will help you choose when light will play an important role and which plants will be affected. Bright sun can illuminate your flowers and foliage, and shade can deepen the color for dramatic affect. You can also use light to create illusions in the garden. Pools and water features can reflect the

Light can also be used in reflection on mirrored surfaces or designs in hardscaping to draw you to a new place in the garden. This dragonfly cutout screams of childhood wonder, forcing you to run up to the fence and see what's on the other side. This infusion of personality mixed with inspiration, wonder, and the functionality of pulling you to a new space in the garden is ingenious.

image of plants nearby. Think of the gorgeous lobed leaves of a Japanese maple (*Amur palmatum*) reflected in the pool of a birdbath in fall. Stunning. Using the architecture of trees, shrubs, or hardscaping can create shadows and movement as an added visual element. Plant a Harry Lauder's walking stick (*Corylus avellana*) next to a wall and, as the sun sets, watch the shadows of the twisted branches dance across the scene. Light isn't just about keeping plants alive. It's about bringing the garden itself alive, an added character to the diverse cast that makes up your landscape.

PAUSE. The final function of plants that I think is important is that of creating moments of pause. So many of us need to be forced to take a breather, and what better place than your outdoor space? Using plants as a tactical way to stop you in your tracks is a much more fun way of doing it than simply putting up a fence to slow you down. This can be done in several ways. Simply by using the size and placement of certain shrubs and trees can force you to change your path, but that's pretty utilitarian. I prefer to create these special moments by engaging the senses. Fragrance is one of the most obvious answers to getting people to stop and ask questions. The staples of gardenia (*Gardenia* spp.), lilac (*Syringa* spp.), wisteria (*Wisteria* spp.), phlox (*Phlox paniculata*), jasmine (*Jasminum* spp.), and lilies (*Lilium* spp.) are joined by a host of other plants that stop you in your tracks and beg to be smelled. It's nostalgic and of the moment, all at once. It may be obvious, but it's impactful. Sightlines, as mentioned above, have a way of drawing people through the space. Whether that's planting a row of plants down a pathway to draw you down or planting a focal point shrub in the far corner of the garden to catch attention, establishing key visual elements, in moderation, gives visual cues for where the visitor should focus and stop to enjoy the garden. Adding water elements or chimes involve your auditory muscles and draw you in, where plants with fuzzy leaves encourage you to touch, and edibles create moments of pause for a nibble as you enjoy the outdoor space. Depending on the scale of your garden, you may not want to incorporate all these elements, but choose what is most important to your goals and aesthetic and what fits within the function of your environment.

What would Martha, Tommy, and Kelly do?

While much of this design element is more about what your garden offers to you and less about personal aesthetic, our friends Kelly, Tommy, and Martha definitely use functionality in their approach to building a landscape. Or at least lay their focus in different areas.

Of everyone, **Kelly** is most likely to incorporate all these functional elements into his design. Remember that his focus is all about embracing the ecology of the existing landscape, so the focus on soil and water would be front and center in his thinking, followed by how to use plant material to augment any challenges that the landscape offers. A diverse plant selection to embrace the existing soil would be an exciting opportunity rather than focusing on amendments.

Tommy's more structured approach would likely utilize hardscaping and a more limited palate to achieve the aesthetic goals of the project while staying in line with water needs of the selected plant material. Tommy would likely focus on the views he's creating, ensuring clean lines drive the view to his desired end point. Tommy is definitely a functional designer at heart, using light and negative space to ground his work.

As **Martha** approaches the functionality of her design, she wants to embrace what the landscape offers, but doesn't mind doing some amendments to achieve her dream aesthetic. Adding some compost or peat moss isn't scary because it might be necessary to get that hydrangea to bloom in sandy soil. Martha would also likely put an emphasis on utility, creating a practical and livable space for her, her family, and friends to enjoy. A little up-front work is an okay thing if it means less maintenance and a more accommodating space in the long run. Native plants likely are a factor here, as sustainability is important to Martha, but may not be the driving force behind all the planting decisions.

Take time to enjoy the view, whether it's one you've created yourself or one provided by Mother Nature.

Shape

It may seem like a duh moment that when we're talking about design, we have to talk about shape. Just like a house, we're building a structure from the under the dirt to above your fence and shapes matter. This is where you get to add definition, add or take away from what already exists in the landscape, and establish the feeling of your landscape. Gardens are about drawing out emotion, and how you design with shape plays a critical role. Just like we talked about with the flare versus skinny jeans in Chapter 1, there's no wrong style. It's just about preference. And those personal preferences start to determine and showcase personality.

The circular front walk of this home embraces a tree, breaking the symmetry of the house.

In garden design, I don't approach shape simply as circle versus triangle. While those help you start to imagine what the garden will look like as plants grow to their mature size, that's just a 2D look at what will be a multi-dimensional living landscape. This element is not just square or oval, big or small. It's about how all those elements come together to elicit reactions to your creativity and work.

SCALE. Instituting size from the outset of your design process will help you fill in the gaps. Understanding scale and proportion, or the size of each object compared to everything around it, will set the structural elements from which you can base the rest of your design. Some of those objects may already exist as established trees, your home or a shed, fences, or buildings in the distance that you want to serve as a far-off focal point. As you layer the garden back from those larger pieces, create a cascading effect that allows you to settle at eye level and that each layer is proportional with the other. If you've got old, established trees, that canopy may not necessarily become a part of the visual design, but it may simply affect the design based on sun exposure and soil concerns. If you're starting more from scratch, you may want to add some of that structure to the corner of the landscape with a noble tree like a maple (*Acer* spp.) or gingko

The repetition of shapes and patterns can help create a cohesive design. Once these new plantings grow in a bit, they will provide the perfect complement to this Tommy-style design.

(*Ginkgo* spp.) or an upright tree like Parkland Pillar birch (*Betula platyphylla*) if you've got less space. From there, you scale down to the shrub or small tree layer, then to the perennial and annual mix, and finally to the groundcover layer. Depending on your design aesthetic, these may blend to achieve a more natural feel, or they may be disparate to be intentionally linear. In any case, be sure to keep in mind the mature size of your plants so that the proportions will ultimately come together.

As you think about scale and plant selection, especially as you tie all this back to budget, remember that you can use larger items such as shrubs and trees to fill space without overplanting. Now, I wouldn't recommend only planting shrubs and trees because you'll lose some of that textural element that I think is so important, but purely focused on scale, having some of those bigger plants helps the budget and creates big moments of impact that visually draw you through the garden.

Speaking of visual impact, playing with scale can be a fun form of trickery. Planting from small to large, or vice versa, or planting from a wide distance to closer distance can feel like it's physically pulling you through the garden. Say you have a long driveway leading up to your house, or a pathway leading to a distant sitting area in your side yard. Using this planting pattern creates a chute-like pathway that piques curiosity enough that you're drawn to the other side. This is where scale has power.

The golden ratio appears in the spiral of this rex begonia (*Begonia rex*) leaf, proportionally spiraling outward from the central stem. Biologically it occurs so that the plant can maximize the leaf's surface space for photosynthesis, but it's also aesthetically appealing to human observers as well, as this pattern appears over and over in nature.

FIBONACCI. I've really tried to keep too much math or science out of this because, if you're anything like me, that's where the words on the page might start to blur a bit. I mentioned the golden ratio in Chapter 1 to talk about the naturally recurring theme that influences architectural design. Well, this golden ratio idea is related to the Fibonacci sequence from a mathematical theory developed by Leonardo of Pisa, where you add the two preceding numbers in the list to determine the next. 0 + 1 = 1, 1 + 1 = 2, 1 + 2 = 3, 2 + 3 = 5, etc. And basically, what these formulas equate to is a spiral-like design that is naturally appealing to us. Because of this, many landscape architects use the Fibonacci sequence or golden ratio calculation to create shapes and scale in their work.

You can do this at home to help figure out the size of your flower beds, choose how many plants should go in each space, and how the heights should relate to each other (throwback to the last section on scale). The general rule of thumb to calculate the size of the flower bed is to decide on at least the long or the short side based on usable space. Multiply the long side by 0.618 or the short side by 1.618, and you'll get the other side's size. For example, if you know you've got 8 feet (2.4 meters) to work with, you multiply that by 0.618 and you get 5 feet (1.5 meters). This pattern of scale is repeated so often in nature that it's something our brain is used to seeing, which is why it helps give us a starting point in bed size.

In addition to using math to create bed sizes, if you look at the Fibonacci sequence, you'll also see numbers that help us with bed design: 1, 2, 3, 5, 8, 13, 21, 34 and so on give a good guideline as to how many of each plant to use. Again, our brains are naturally aligned with this sequence, so when planting in small numbers or in mass, stick to those listed by Leonardo of Pisa as a guide and you're off to the races.

PATTERN. As you use the Fibonacci sequence in your planting design (it's also a bonus fun fact for cocktail parties), this will help you start to set the rhythm of your design. Unless you're creating a showcase garden for unique species and planting one of each variety, planting in groups will make the landscape flow more naturally and be more visually exciting. Creating patterns by massing plants in numbers listed above is a functional start to the process, but then start adding in some of the other design elements that we've discussed: color, texture, and seasonality. Where will you see pops of spring color or swells of fall ornamental grasses? How do those seasonal elements play with the neighboring plants? While you're creating blocks of individual plant varieties, you're really creating plant communities made up of these individual elements, and they have to work together to feel like a cohesive space. Start drawing out the blocks of plants from an aerial view so you can start to see the plant communities, but always remember the

Circular shapes in the landscape evoke a feeling of structured movement. Use the Fibonacci sequence as a guideline for scale.

The patterns and groupings of plants in this garden create cohesiveness that holds this minimalist design together.

drawing is a 2D starting place, and you'll want to envision in 3D before you start buying anything (I'll share some examples of these 2D drawings later in this section).

As you're choosing plants to create these patterns, think about which are your primary varieties and colors. Adding repetition of these plants and echoes of color brings a cohesiveness to your design, simplifies your process, and continues to drive the personality of the garden. If you're repeating bright red coneflowers (*Echinacea* spp.) throughout the garden, that's a totally different feeling than a more muted moon garden filled with white blooms. If you love purple, be sure that you're echoing that color throughout the space with complementary or a triad of colors mixed in. The varieties don't have to be repeated necessarily, but repetition of color will also set the rhythm of the garden.

BALANCE. The final piece of advice that I have for you as we wrap up the elements of design is that everything must flow together and create balance. I've shared too many ideas to fit into one individual landscape and capture your personal aesthetic and goals. As you pare down what matters most to you and what elements you choose for your outdoor space, think about how everything works with the other pieces of the puzzle. Remember how we talked about feng shui in Chapter 1? This is where the rubber meets the road. Think of the five elements of that design principle—earth, fire, wood, water, and metal—and bring it outside. How do your plants meld with your hardscaping, water features, art, or existing trees? Are you featuring what is most important to you? All the elements must come together to create the feeling of the space for which you are aiming. As you sit down with your pencil and start sketching and listing out plants and hardscaping materials, have the final thought be about this balance.

What would Martha, Tommy, and Kelly do?

As you're pondering, let me give you one more thing to consider. Do you prefer everything to be in symmetry, or are you comfortable with moments of asymmetry? This goes back to our conversation about harmony versus tension. If you're creating a zen space, building in tension with dense plantings of various textures, narrowing pathways, or sectional color differences wouldn't be for you. On the flipside, if you like a bit of controlled chaos in a more natural setting, choosing vertical structured plants in a monochromatic color scheme might be too harmonious. If you're comfortable with tension or asymmetry, there are ways to build it to have a balanced resolution. To do this, you use color, texture, size, and focal points to create the illusion of asymmetrical or informal balance. Taller plants placed near the back of the garden may seem to have similar weight as a shorter, wider plant placed near the front. Darker colors seem heavier than lighter colors, so to create balance, you might need to add more of the lighter plants. Broadleaf plants may feel bigger than those with fine needles or thin leaves, so you may need to bulk up the daintier foliage plants to add balance. Again, this isn't about creating mirror images throughout the landscape, but creating the illusion of harmony.

Shape is the design element that **Tommy** absolutely lives for in his work. Structure and scale and balance are the heartbeat of his gardens. Following the structure of the golden ratio and Fibonacci sequence, creating symmetry, and using scale to manipulate the aesthetic make him so happy.

Surprisingly, our friend **Kelly**, who usually uses a differing approach than Tommy, is in lock step here. Because Kelly prefers a looser aesthetic, having a structured approach to shape is important so that the design doesn't get messy and overcrowded. Repetition in Fibonacci numbers adds comprehension to a garden that could quickly devolve into chaos. So, as we round out our design process, Kelly and Tommy come together.

Martha is likely a pretty close rule follower here too. Because this focus on shape ultimately forms the experience and feeling of the garden, she wouldn't stray too far from the basic principles. She would likely stick closer to a symmetrical design but may add some asymmetrical elements in using a focal point to draw her guests toward a cocktail patio that she created in an unseen part of the garden behind a hedge row. Just because she generally creates a more classic design doesn't mean that she doesn't infuse personality into her space. She's an entertainer, after all!

Use patterns and symmetry to create a harmonious garden and keep things from getting too messy or overcrowded. But too much of both may be too rigid for some gardeners. Find a level of each that appeals to you.

Put It On Paper

I've thrown a lot of theory and hypothetical at you. So, before we get into specific case studies to showcase Martha, Tommy, and Kelly's aesthetics in specific designs, let's look at how these concepts can fit across any lot size. You don't necessarily have to hire a fancy designer to lay out your outdoor space as long as you know these foundational principles. Start with existing structures and hardscaping goals, then build in layers of plant material from large to small, matching your landscape's cultural needs (remember sun exposure, soil, and so on from our date days).

As you review these illustrations, think of the concepts from the first few chapters and how they apply to your specific place. As you align with your design personality, I hope you're inspired by each of these plans to start building out a plan for home, and then fill in plants as you get into the recipe cards in Chapter 5. Grab some pencils—don't be scared to mess up and erase—and start sketching out the general design for what you want your outdoor space to look like when you have your friends over. Then dive into each case study to see how I plan outdoor spaces for each design personality. Happy planning!

A top-down view of your space that includes the footprint of the garden, your home, and any other structures is a great way to play with design possibilities. If you don't have a drone to get a shot like this one of a yard in the American Southwest, sketch your space out on paper and start roughing out possible designs.

Small Site

Martha

This small site is designed for Martha. Notice the curved lines of the beds and the classic hardscapes. The raised vegetable beds and arbor at the back of the yard add further functionality, an important trait for a Martha garden.

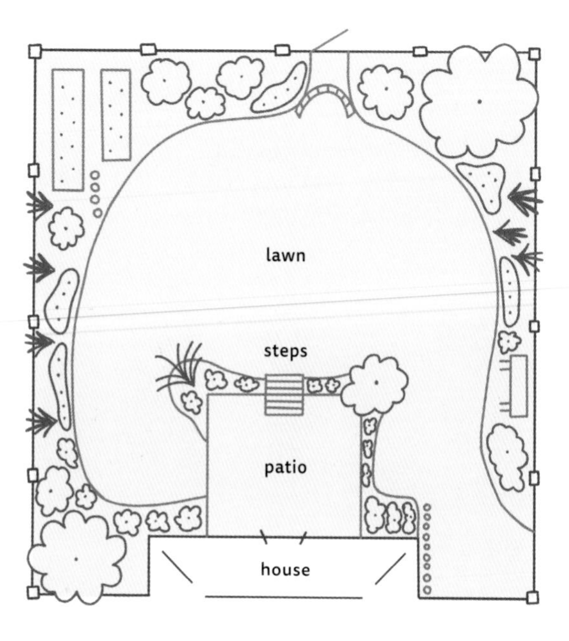

Tommy

The same small site is now designed with Tommy in mind. The straight lines, linear flow, and rigid hardscape elements are a perfect fit for his minimalist style. The plants are in straight rows and the edges of beds are crisp.

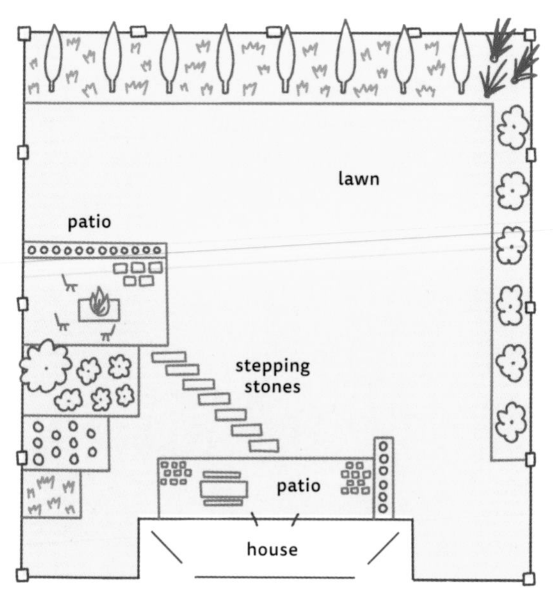

Kelly

And here is the same small site designed for Kelly. This naturalistic design contains curving edges and a mixture of perennials and grasses, combined with a few small trees and shrubs. Everything is mingling together and the natural stone patio fits in perfectly.

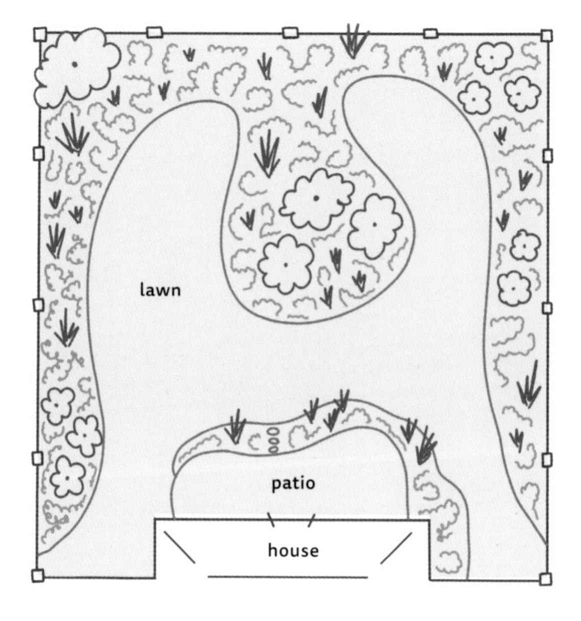

Medium Site

Martha

This illustration shows a medium-sized yard designed for the ever-refined Martha. Evergreen hedges line the front walk, and perennials and shrubs combine together to make a harmonious and classic design. The edges are soft, with the front yard and back yard complementing each other beautifully.

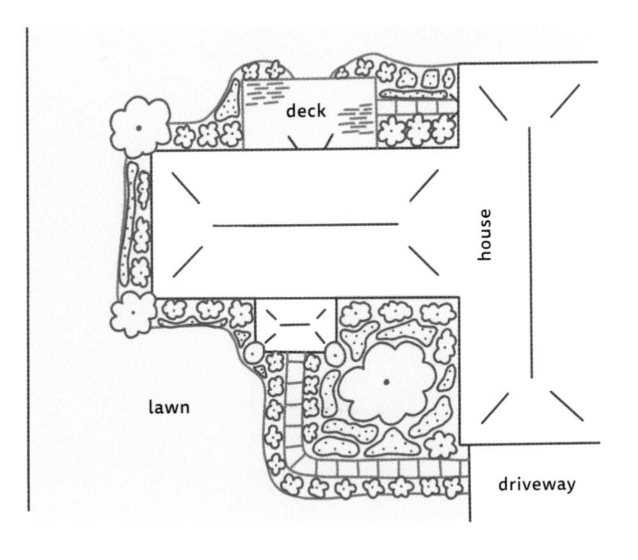

Tommy

The same medium-sized site is now designed with Tommy in mind. There is a more rigid structure overall, with plants placed in straight rows, clean lines, and open views. The rectangular patio pavers tie the front yard to the back seamlessly.

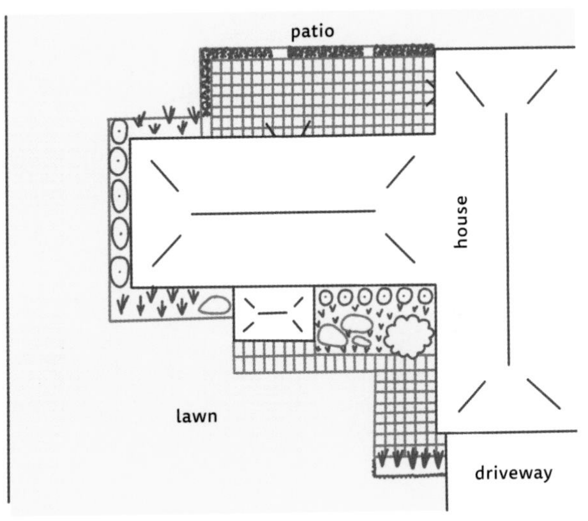

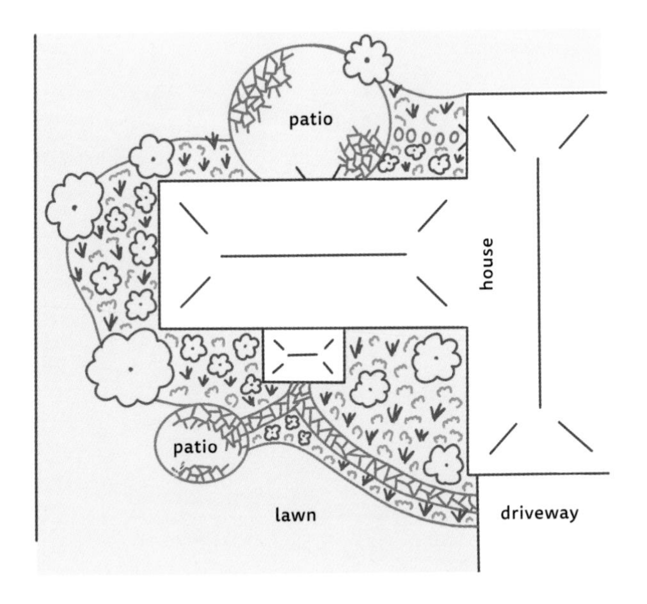

Kelly

For Kelly, this medium-sized yard means the opportunity for playful curves and mingled plantings. The flagstone walk and patios are surrounded by a prairie-like mixture of native perennials, grasses, shrubs, and small trees. The round front patio is perfect for evening cocktails or morning coffee.

Large Site

Martha

A large site designed for Martha contains a curved stone patio and front walkway. Plants like perennials and shrubs are placed in small groups of 3, 5, or 7 plants with uniformity, structure, and balance. The front of the house has a classic hedge of flowering or evergreen shrubs under the picture window, and the far right corner is host to a small weeping tree.

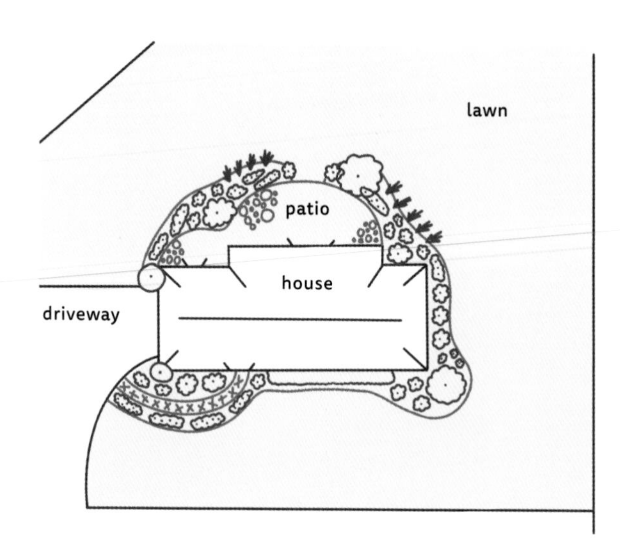

Tommy

In Tommy's eyes, the same large site is better suited to a far smaller number of plant species planted in greater numbers. Rigid lines of plants and a simple concrete patio fit his aesthetics perfectly. An evergreen groundcover underlies taller plants to reduce weeding and provide winter interest.

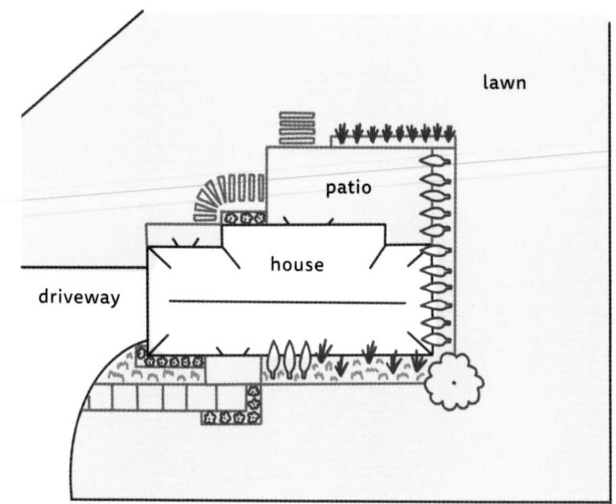

Kelly

When this large site is designed to please Kelly, it is a happy jumble of intentionally placed plants with natural stepping stones inviting you to the front door. The back patio is shaped to mimic a pond, with grasses along the outer edge. Big planting beds mean more bees, butterflies, and ladybugs.

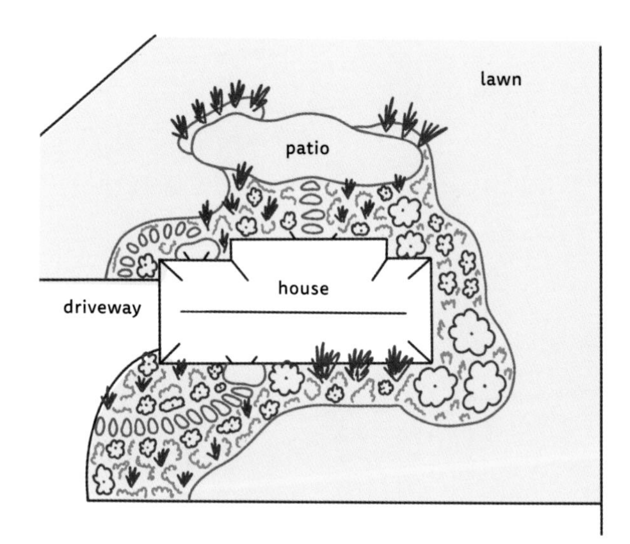

Case Studies

"Education is the kindling of a flame, not the filling of a vessel."

—SOCRATES

Before we go one word further, take a breather. You just took in a mountain of information, especially if you're new in this whole gardening world. I threw a lot at you. New terms, concepts, plant names, math problems . . . Now before we jump into recipes of plant combinations for your landscape, I want to give some real-life examples of how each of our aesthetic guides from Chapter 4 could bring those design elements to life. As you read through each case study, reflect on everything you've learned throughout the book and pair that with how the designers are solving problems for their landscape. By the end, you should be fairly certain which is most relevant to you. Now, it's totally fine to pick and choose from more than one, but you'll likely see a more dominant character come through to help you make plant choices in Chapter 5.

The dichotomy of the natural-tone planter against the cool tones of the siding draws your eye to this lush tropical display.

MARTHA
The Classic

Our fictional character Martha is going to help my real-life friends Casey and Andy with their new home landscape plan. As a reminder, Martha's style is refined, trends toward mixed-use spaces, focuses on easy maintenance, and is what you'd imagine in an elevated suburban setting. Casey and Andy have two small children and purchased their home within the past year. There is some existing landscaping, but it's a pretty limited and disjointed place from which to start.

Stage 1: The existing garden

THE GOAL. These two are some of my favorite people. They have such a cute young family, are super active, and love to entertain. With that, they're really busy all the time and want a beautiful landscape, but don't have a ton of time to maintain it. They're willing to put in the work but aren't necessarily wanting to be out there every day to keep it looking nice. The home they bought is in a lovely suburban neighborhood where people keep up their houses and yards, invest in the community, and live there for the long haul. It's pretty darn idyllic, but what I love about it is that everyone likes to add some personality, so each house is a little bit different. One neighbor has a yellow door, the other a turf-less front lawn full of pollinator plants. It's funky and fun.

Along those lines, Casey and Andy don't want a cookie cutter landscape design; they want to infuse some personality into their whole home. They're painting trim, updating house numbers, replacing decking, and digging out overgrown shrubs. Now they want some fresh plant material to give the landscape a facelift to match their cute house. The look should be refined like Martha, with a dash of spice and four-season interest. Living in the Midwest, they want to take advantage of the seasons and choose plants that honor even the coldest of days. And remember, two small children plus a social life means not overdoing it on the maintenance. Challenge accepted.

KEY ELEMENTS. To set the stage, this project takes place in a moderate climate where the front of the landscape faces east-southeast. That means that it gets a lot of sun in the morning, and by afternoon it's starting to get blocked by mature trees and the house. They've got pretty decent soil, but it can trend a bit clay heavy. This means that we'll need to select plants that can tolerate a bit more water near their roots or we'll have to do some amending to get some of Casey and Andy's favorite plants in the mix.

First and foremost, every plant selected needs to be low maintenance. Some seasonal pruning or fertilizer application is okay, but we can't go beyond that to support their lifestyle. We'll trend more toward shrubs and ornamental grasses so there is less work to do throughout the year, though we may add some bulbs to give their garden an early jumpstart.

Because they like to entertain, we will include a variation of plant species so there's always something to enjoy in the garden, like a fresh-cut bouquet indoors or on the deck. This diversity of material will also support their goal of having a four-season garden. Their winters can get cold—10 degrees Fahrenheit (-23 degrees Celsius), so there is great opportunity for some fall and winter color.

This garden also should have plants that engage all the senses. Their kids are super curious about the outdoors, so giving them plants that satisfy that interest will be an added fun bonus. Plants with fuzzy leaves, seed heads, fragrance, and unique flowers are a must. Along those lines, their family likes to eat healthy and cook from scratch. So, we'll be incorporating edibles into the mix in the fenced-in backyard. It may seem like a lot of elements to include, but by creating phases in the planting schedule, they can tackle the installation project on weekends over a couple of months.

DESIGN STRATEGY. Driven by the goals and climate for Casey and Andy, we'll focus on three of our key design elements: color, seasonality, and shape. Using these as the guiding light for our process will direct the scope and parameters for plant selection.

With a neutral siding color, that leaves a lot of room for exploration, as well as established beds along the front sidewalk and at the end of their driveway. To tie this all together, we will connect the bed near the street and that on the near side of the sidewalk by creating a rounded bed all along the driveway to create separation between the concrete and the turf lawn, as well as make the planting beds cohesive. Near the street, we'll keep the stonecrop (*Sedum* spp.) for fall color and because it can handle the salt from the plow in winter, and then add low-growing perennial geraniums (*Geranium* spp.) for summer blooms that will fill in the gaps before the stonecrop arrives later in the season. Along the driveway, we'll continue the blue-purple swatch with additional salt-tolerant perennials, such as catmint (*Nepeta* spp.) and clustered bellflower (*Campanula glomerata*) accented by pops of yellow daylilies (*Hemerocallis* spp.).

As we near the house, we'll build a bed that's a bit larger in size, so that the eye is naturally drawn toward the front door as the welcome place. The yellow daylilies will continue on the back side of the sidewalk and will be echoed by the mounded Cobalt-n-Gold hypericum (*Hypericum kalmianum*) near the front of the driveway. This adds structure but hides the sidewalk from the street and transitions the primary color to the yellow flowers of the hypericum. Along the front porch, behind the yellow daylilies, will be a short hedge row of compact panicle hydrangeas—we're using Little Hottie (*Hydrangea paniculata* 'Bailpanone')—which will bloom white in summer and provide a crisp backdrop to the yellow and purple in front. We'll amend the soil with some gypsum to break up the clay and allow for water to drain more freely and create a moist versus wet soil. Past the front door will be the largest shrubs, as we've built in waves from the road to the house from smallest to largest. Between the windows will be an upright lilac (*Syringa x*) to anchor the foundation of the home, bring an early pop of purple color to usher in the color palette before the perennial geranium blooms, and add fragrance to the front of the house so that when Casey, Andy, and their kids have the windows open in spring they'll enjoy the fragrance of lilacs wafting in. Underneath each window will be dwarf fountain grass (*Pennisetum alopecuroides* 'Hameln') to carry the fall flavor back from the stonecrop in front and marry well with the parchment-colored fall blooms of the panicle hydrangea. The grasses, panicle hydrangeas, and stonecrop will give great architecture to the winter garden, and to fill in the gaps in spring while the ornamental grass and panicle hydrangeas aren't showing off, sprinkles of early-blooming bulbs will be planted throughout to ensure that all four seasons are well represented.

FINAL IMPLICATIONS. When making this planting design, the focus was providing complementary colors, multi-season interest, and no headaches with plant maintenance. Not only did we accomplish that, but we were able to add continuity to the space by connecting the planting beds with colorful, salt-tolerant plants that can thrive in full sun and with wet feet. Casey, Andy, and the kids can be proud of their new front entrance and enjoy it year-round.

Stage 2: The ouline of the new planting beds

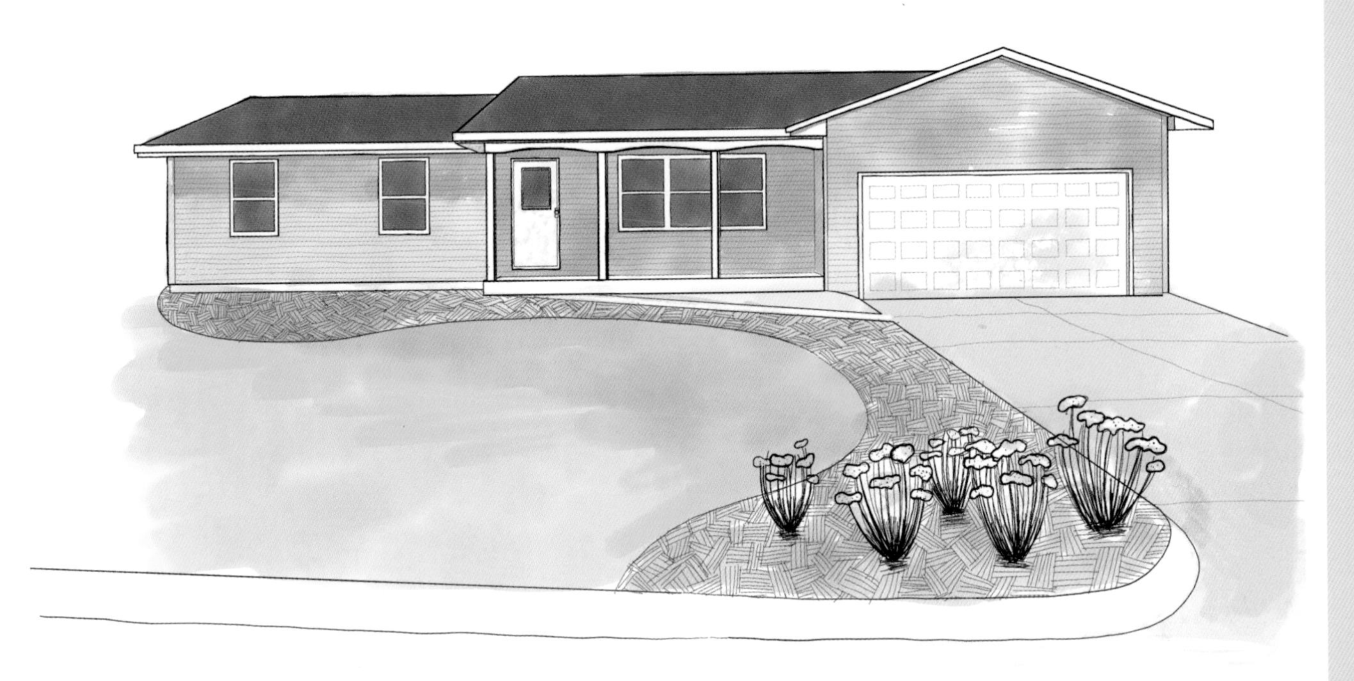

Stage 3: The fully planted landscape

TOMMY
The Minimalist

My friends Chad and Mark have the most beautiful midcentury modern home that I absolutely drool over. The architecture, the color scheme, and the towering oaks in back are like a dream come true. They have put a lot of work into this house, both with the interior and exterior, and so they are looking to capitalize on Tommy's design style to make some small tweaks to bring their landscape up to snuff with the rest of the house.

Stage 1: The existing garden

THE GOAL. Chad and Mark are already starting off on a great foot. The house is beautiful, and the landscaping is good. Our goal is to get them to great. Both are highly successful professionals who like to entertain, so the vibe is classy and upscale without being overdone. They don't mind paying for a little bit of maintenance, so the opportunity for some seasonal displays is ideal, especially for when visitors arrive. Like the rest of the landscape design, the seasonal installations should be sleek and polished without going overboard.

We should also be sure that the design fits the modern aesthetic of the house, maintains strong balance, and keeps the color scheme restrained. While the house is surrounded in green, the more natural and dark tones of the paint and hardscaping provide a nice contrast that should be maintained. This project does not call for a lot of color, but rather an accent to the focal point, which is the home itself. This is all about sharp visuals, a photo-worthy entrance, uncluttered design, and seasonal accents to entertain visitors.

KEY ELEMENTS. Chad and Mark live in a temperate climate where winters don't traditionally get below zero and frost isn't a major issue. Their house faces west and has a big grove of established noble trees in back, so the sun exposure is in the afternoon. The soil is a sandy loam, which is pretty ideal. All in all, this is a great site, especially for a homeowner who isn't focused on flower power, which requires a bit more sun.

In designing this project, Tommy would start by reviewing the lines of the home and hardscaping to make sure that the planting plan complements it. With this modern approach, we don't want to create a lot of discord so we will focus on creating balance. Reviewing the existing planting plus the architecture of the home, the clean lines are evident, but the balance is a bit off as everything is weighted toward the front entrance. The existing decorative containers are symmetrical, but the remainder of the design is not. This will be a key to moving this good landscape to great.

The current design shows mostly a monoculture, or planting of a single species, of Karl Foerster feather reed grass (*Calamagrostis x acutiflora*). This singular approach is fitting for a modern, minimalistic aesthetic, but we can amp it up a bit by creating a bit more diversity to add some multi-season texture and color.

Because this is an entertainer's home, we do want to be sure that lighting and hardscaping are smartly placed and intact, matched well with the live plants. The idea of clean lines should continue through these tactile pieces and amplify the beauty of the home.

DESIGN STRATEGY. For Chad and Mark, this approach is all about the design elements of scale, pattern, and harmony. This is Tommy's sweet spot.

Knowing that we've got some strong bones to start with, let's start with scale. Since the trees are so large in the background, we'll focus on the line of sight. The green shield is just a blur that gives us a colorful palette to paint on but not necessarily engage with as we look at scale and proportions. The height of the existing ornamental grass is pretty nice, but gaining a bit of height to reach the lower roof line would tie everything together nicely. Look for a large shrub or small tree, such as a compact crape myrtle (*Lagerstroemia* spp.), star magnolia (*Magnolia stellata*), or Crimson Queen Japanese maple (*Acer palmatum var. dissectum* 'Crimson Queen') to plant in the center of that block of Karl Foerster feather reed grass to add height, structure, texture, and additional fall color that will complement the deep tones of the home. Additionally, using annuals around the grass is lovely, and I would recommend cycling additional plants into the mix, starting off the season with white tulips followed by the orange marigolds and underplanted with the grass, which will be cut back in spring. That will give the entire bed color that will shine against the dark siding. As the tulips fade, your compact tree will start to fill out for summer followed by the fall show of ornamental grasses. All while looking refined and clever.

Because the planting is so heavily weighted outside the front door, the balance is a bit off. To create harmony and symmetry, which is key to this modern and minimalist design style, we will create a matching, albeit slightly smaller, bed on the opposite side of the driveway. Because the concrete is poured to match the smaller garage door, we don't want it exactly matching, but the echo of replicated plant palette will provide a more cohesive look.

Stage 2: The ouline of the new planting beds

Finally, the decorative pots themselves are gorgeous, but the draping annuals are a mismatch with the rest of the design. This is where you can continue your focus on seasonal displays, similar to the tulips in the ground, and add additional height and rigid structure. Since they live in a warmer climate, utilizing plants such as agave (*Agave* spp.), snake plant (*Dracaena trifasciata*), or green aloe (*Furcraea foetida*) would act as a nice pairing with the tree.

FINAL IMPLICATIONS. Though we didn't need to do much editing, adding the second flower bed, earlier pops of seasonal color with tulip bulbs, and elevating the overall sightline with a compact tree makes this design really stand out. Adding some balance to the planting plan without overloading plants or hardscaping fits the chic vibe and makes the design more complete.

Stage 3: The fully planted landscape

KELLY
The Naturalist

As I've mentioned throughout the book, my fiancé (now husband) and I purchased a 1979 rambler that had just been flipped in early 2021. They did a great job inside the house, but what hooked us and made us put in an offer that same day was the almost half-acre lot (which was impossible to find in our area at that price point) that was adjacent to a city park and nature reserve. Most of our lot was behind the house and backed up to a pond. When the previous owner was updating the home, he took out the junk trees and overgrown shrubs, leaving us with a beautiful vista of established trees and wide-open space to build a garden. It was a perfect, south-facing bowl in which I could create a beautiful forever-home landscape. Finally, no more tiny, north-facing, middle townhome unit, tree root-filled blip of dirt! I was ready and raring to go. The only problem was that it was January in Minnesota with regular temperatures well below zero degrees. But that gave me a few months to make a really solid staged plan for planting. So, for our last case study, let's dive a bit deeper into my own planting plan.

Stage 1: The existing garden

THE GOAL. In years past, I may have leaned toward a more modern approach to design, but my taste has really evolved to a more naturalized aesthetic. As my dear friend Kelly Norris—the inspiration behind "The Naturalist"—articulates in his book *New Naturalism*, this trend toward planting for your place to work *with* nature without fighting it is not only ecologically important but can provide a more beautiful planting with less maintenance. I also loved the idea of having a full, lush, textured garden without relying on mulch to fill open spaces. A densely planted landscape would give me a beautiful foreground to the trees and pond behind, provide a more sustainable solution, and fill our cold-climate garden with four seasons of beauty.

Beyond the area that would become the garden, my goal was to reduce our footprint of turf grass and fix some other underlying issues later discovered in the lawn itself. The house is in the woods, so I wanted to bring us back into that feeling versus a suburban home with a rigid landscape plan. It was time to dig in.

KEY ELEMENTS. While my intention was not to create a fully native landscape, the importance of place that Kelly describes in his book was still important. I wanted to mimic some of the wild elements set as the backdrop in the park reserve and create additional pops of color and texture with a number of non-native species, such as roses and hydrangeas, in my cold-climate garden. These are woven into the design to maintain the wilder aspects of a naturalistic planting and the benefits of a native ecosystem. I definitely wasn't creating an old English rose garden, but with the right plant pairings, even some more of those traditional plants can weave into a naturalistic plant palette.

Because the plants will trend toward a subtle mix of native and non-native species, I want to be sure the hardscaping matches that feel. Choosing more natural tones and rough-cut pieces fits the vibe of our woods much better than slate tiles. Because much of our property is in the woods, we need to pay attention to the light and how it dances over the lawn at different times of year. At least twice a week, I took photos of the yard to see how much sun exposure everything gets in spring before the trees fill in versus summer when the stand of mature trees is fully leafed out. That has big impact on what we choose for each season of growth.

Finally, my goal is to create an interactive landscape. It's my first real home garden, so I want it to be lush and full and something that I can work in and enjoy on a regular basis. It's a place for learning and education and trying new plants. There will be great density but also the understanding that some things will work, and others won't, but that means I get to try something new. This garden is a place for the unique and interesting, where we will experiment and celebrate discovery.

DESIGN STRATEGY. The process of creating this planting plan was both exhilarating and daunting since I was starting from scratch on such a big lot. We have two dogs and a lot of wildlife coming in and out from the park, so setting boundaries for a new fence was step one. We opted for black chain link since it would all be planted, and we didn't want to block the view of the pond with a privacy fence. This would also set up guardrails for where I would build the deepest bones of the garden. Determining where the fence would be installed was not just determined by our property line, but with the awareness of the massive deer pressure. We left some space behind the fence to plant some tough hedge plants—we used Straight Talk® privet (*Ligustrum vulgare*), a variety with little to no seed set—that would be out of sight from the house and yard, and we didn't mind if the deer used as a snack because it would hold them back from eating our more tender and appetizing shrubs and trees.

Once the fence and our back border was set, it was time to dig into the bigger shrubs and trees since we had 200 linear feet (61 meters) to plant. As mentioned in Chapter 4, we started with water-wise shrubs such as Fiber Optics buttonbush (*Cephalanthus occidentalis*) and Firedance dogwood (*Cornus sericea*) to soak up the wet part of the new garden bed. From there, we added additional anchoring shrubs such as pearlbush (*Exochorda x macrantha*), sageleaf willow (*Salix candida*), and ninebark (*Physocarpus opulifolius*) before building ornamental grasses and perennials. The initial design plan for the first 35 feet (just over 10 meters) called for over 100 plants. This may seem like a lot but remember it's a dense planting to maximize all four seasons in our cold climate, with the intention that plants will intertwine to show off their best assets.

There is more to come, including a full bulb planting strategy under the tree canopy that allows for mostly full, filtered sunlight all spring before filtered shade in summer, as well as converting our now-dead turf front lawn into a pollinator haven. Check out my Instagram (@ryanplantsplants) for all the updates!

Stage 2: The ouline of the new planting beds

FINAL IMPLICATIONS. While this is still a work in progress, the initial plan for this space is structured wildness. We're embracing the tree canopy and park behind us, including native and new introductions, and allowing the garden to creep into the lawn. Despite the heat and drought of summer, most of the new plants have survived and are adapting because many are native to this region. As the garden fills in, it will be full of texture, personality, and create memorable views that beg for their photo to be taken. As I continue to experience my new yard, I look forward to the challenge of finding even more unique plants to get in the ground and show off to anyone who visits.

Stage 3: The fully planted landscape

5

Recipe Cards

"Oh, the places you'll go!"

—DR. SEUSS

PARTY TIME HAS ARRIVED! I've already given some ideas for plant selection, but now is where it all comes full circle and we get to start putting it all together. You've learned a lot over the past four chapters, so I know that you'll be able to search online or head to your local garden center and understand how to start using the plants in your own garden. However, I want to finish the book with some specific inspiration. I can't leave you hanging! As you dig through these recipes and start putting them to use in the real world, remember that these are all general guidelines for success. It's a framework for concepts that will help you build the landscape of your dreams.

As you work your way through Chapter 5, you'll see that I've organized these recipes by style according to our friends **Martha**, **Kelly**, and **Tommy**, and then by climate. While this is supposed to narrow focus a bit, I still urge you to read through everything. You've made it this far—don't skip ahead! So many of these plants fit into multiple categories, so just because something shows up in Kelly's design palette for a moderate climate doesn't necessarily mean it won't work for Martha in a cold climate. After the recipe cards, you'll find a handful of additional plant charts to help you make plant selections based on your particular design style.

Keep your notes from previous chapters handy: You've got some digging to do and plants to install. Creating a planning and design checklist will help you synthesize everything you've learned: how much space you want to fill, how the sun and soil affect plant selection, how to plan for mature plant size, how to play with color and texture, relying on Fibonacci, what style best fits your vision, and so much more. Pour a cup of coffee or glass of wine and buckle in for the end of the ride. It's the moment you've been waiting for the whole book. It's plant time, friend!

MARTHA
The Classic

We're starting with Martha because she will have the most plants that will overlap with Kelly and Tommy. Everyone can learn a little something from Martha. Refined beauty with a dollop of personality and fun. We'll start with plants that do well in the cold and make our way through dry, arid heat to those in the subtropics and beyond.

For those of you who live in climates like me with cold, sometimes brutal winters, we need some pretty tough plants, but we can still have amazingly beautiful gardens, albeit with shorter growing seasons. Many times, I get asked what we can even grow in our "frozen tundra," but the answer is that we have some spectacular plants that thrive, even with temperatures that reach to -20 or -30 degrees Fahrenheit (-34 Celsius). Martha's classic style focuses on rock-solid shrubs and trees as the foundation of her planting and accents with cold-hardy perennials and bulbs to make the landscape sumptuous and photo-ready. As you work your way to warmer climates, the plant palette opens up and offers an even wider array of plants to play with as you plan. From the cottage garden to edibles, there is so much to explore. In arid or high elevation climates, Martha's focus on solid plants that don't need a ton of maintenance continues. Let's dig in.

Roses, campanula, clematis and other classic cottage-style plants are the cherries on top of a Martha garden.

Star magnolia (*Magnolia stellata*)

Hoary vervain (*Verbena stricta*)

Pink Sparkler birchleaf spirea (*Spiraea betulifolia*)

RECIPE CARD

REGION Cold climate (Down to -30°F / -34°C)
STYLE Martha: The Classic
GOAL Maximize full sun with well-drained soil

This combination lets different characters play the leading role at different times of year. In spring, the magnolia takes center stage with its soft pink blooms, which are then echoed in late spring and early summer by the spirea's protrusion of pink flowers. Using an analogous approach to color, planting vervain continues to brighten the space with purple flowers that sneak up behind the spirea in summer, adding a spiky texture in front of the green leaves of the magnolia. To complete the design, add Hakone grass in front to echo the spiky shape of the vervain, but with a swooping downward motion to ground the planting with soft arching leaves framing the star of the show. As the vervain blooms fade in early fall, Pink Sparkler spirea will again push out pink blooms, this time all the way down the stem, and the leaves will turn a deep burgundy as the Hakone grass changes to copper.

Hakone grass (*Hakonechloa macra*)

RECIPE CARD

REGION Cold climate (Down to -30°F / -34°C)
STYLE Martha: The Classic
GOAL Fill part shade and clay soil with seasonal color

Planting in clay generally presents a challenge, but taking away the sun adds another layer of complexity in a cold climate garden. This combination takes those worries away in a second and adds multi-season color, bold leaves to brighten a shady spot, and fabulous texture. As the ground starts to thaw in spring, the fronds of your fern will start to emerge like a prehistoric beast awakening from their slumber. I love using ferns because they're a great way to fill negative space and add textured green as a backdrop to the rest of the planting. As the fronds start to unfurl, your azalea will pop with early season color like fireworks in the shade. As the azalea blooms fade and leaves fill in, so will the large leaves of Fire and Ice hosta, which has beautiful white and green variegation to add summer-long brightness. And speaking of summer, adding 'Bottle Rocket' leopard plant to the mix brings more large leaves, but with a serrated edge to mimic the cut leaves of the fern with the most gorgeous yellow flowers standing densely upright in the part shade garden.

Ostrich fern (*Matteuccia struthiopteris*)

'Fire and Ice' hosta (*Hosta*)

Azalea (*Rhododendron*)

'Bottle Rocket' leopard plant (*Ligularia stenocephala*)

Easy Elegance Kashmir rose (*Rosa* 'BAImir')

First Editions Vanilla Strawberry panicle hydrangea (*Hydrangea paniculata* 'Renhy')

Little Galaxy African lily (*Agapanthus* hybrid)

RECIPE CARD

REGION **Temperate climate (Down to -5°F / -21°C)**

STYLE **Martha: The Classic**

GOAL **Create layers in full sun with sandy loam soil**

There's very little that's more classic than hydrangeas and roses and combining them in the garden is nostalgic and reminiscent of a beautiful English cottage garden. Adding the African lily and annual purslane to the mix completes the triad of color as well as adds the expected layers of this style of garden, with the orange purslane flowers hugging the ground followed by the blue blooms of the African lily rising just above before reaching the red rose and white summer blooms of the panicle hydrangea. I've selected Little Galaxy African lily because it's a bit more cold tolerant and compact than the species. It also plays well with the hydrangea, which will start to fade to pink as the summer evenings cool into fall temperatures. The shrub rose will continue blooming until frost, so the garden will remain lush throughout the season. Mixing in an annual such as Mojave tangerine is fun because you can try new plants each year, but since it's not a big shrub or hefty perennial, it's not a lot of work to clean up and plant again.

Mojave tangerine purslane (*Portulaca umbraticola*)

RECIPE CARD

REGION Temperate climate (Down to -5°F / -21°C)
STYLE Martha: The Classic
GOAL Achieve classic cottage garden style

The cottage garden is one of the most classic and photographed styles of design. While it may trend toward Kelly's structured unstructured style, the cottage garden is a surprisingly planful and intentional planting process, so I'm giving this one to Martha. While it feels loose, the cottage garden design is all about a charming space that celebrates colorful plants. For those of you lucky enough to live in temperate climates, I've selected a play on blue and deep pink for this plan. For a cottage garden, you'll choose a lot more plants to fill the space, but these four varieties will give you a foundation from which you can build out your landscape. Hydrangeas are a classic plant, and by using a reblooming variety, you'll get fresh color from early summer through fall. Be sure not to prune this one; just deadhead the first set of blooms in mid to late summer and you'll maximize your flower power. The Russian sage adds to the cool tones, which are offset by the pink of My Girl rose—another classic species in the cottage garden—and a pink garden phlox like Bubblegum Pink (*Phlox paniculata* 'Ditomfra').

Endless Summer The Original Hydrangea (*Hydrangea macrophylla* 'Bailmer')

Garden phlox (*Phlox paniculata*)

Russian sage (*Salvia yangii*)

Easy Elegance My Girl rose (*Rosa* 'BAIgirl')

Sweet Tea gardenia (*Gardenia jasminoides* 'PIIGA-II')

Fairy fan flower (*Scaevola aemula*)

RECIPE CARD

REGION **Subtropic climate (Down to 20°F / -6°C)**
STYLE **Martha: The Classic**
GOAL **Build beautiful container combinations**

Building container gardens is an especially fun project because you get to create unique moments of beauty. For this design plan, I am only focusing on three varieties, one of which will play with the other two. Decorative containers are a great way to add color to an otherwise vacant place in the landscape, possibly on a hard surface, or in quiet parts of the garden. I would use the gardenia and ti plant as individual focal points and repeat those pots throughout your space, and then add the fairy fan flower as a trailing bloomer over the edge of both pots. This adds continuity to the design while also allowing you to build upward with the fan of the ti plant and add fragrance to the space with the gardenia. As an added bonus, Sweet Tea is a reblooming gardenia, so you'll have those white blooms and the beautiful smell all summer long.

Ti plant (*Cordyline fruticosa*)

RECIPE CARD

REGION Subtropic climate (Down to 20°F / -6°C)
STYLE Martha: The Classic
GOAL Create a beautiful, yet functional edible garden

Typically, I like to mix edibles and ornamental plants together, but moving to the subtropics opens doors that we just don't have in Minnesota. Because edibles aren't just for food and are beautiful plants as well, we can create an entirely ornamental landscape with food crops. I love the idea of putting a lemon tree in a terra cotta pot on a patio and then building a small (ornamental) edible garden around that corner. Peach Sorbet blueberry also can be grown in a pot or in the ground, even in this warm climate. It is bred to stay compact and beautiful, so it's a fabulous addition to a home landscape. Basil brings us a bit closer to ground level, giving us levels to make a coherent design. I love Amazel Basil because it has fabulous downy mildew resistance. Not only does this keep the plant edible, but it keeps the look of your garden much cleaner. Finally, strawberries are fabulous groundcovers and should be used more regularly in landscape design. Berried Treasure red is a fabulous selection that has gorgeous red flowers and delicious berries that spread along the soil.

Berried Treasure red strawberry (*Fragaria x ananassa*)

Meyer lemon tree (*Citrus x meyeri*)

Amazel Basil sweet Italian basil (*Ocimum* hybrid)

Peach Sorbet blueberry bush (*Vaccinium corymbosum* 'ZF06-043')

Manzanita (*Arctostaphylos* spp.)

Torch aloe (*Aloe arborescens*)

Wall germander (*Teucrium chamadrys*)

Indian hawthorn (*Rhaphiolepis indica*)

RECIPE CARD

REGION	Arid or high elevation climate (Less than 10 inches / 25 cm of annual rainfall or elevation above 5,000 feet / 1,524 meters)
STYLE	Martha: The Classic
GOAL	Create a design to enjoy at a winter home in the desert

Being from the Midwest, a lot of friends and family move to warmer climates for the winter months, so a winter home isn't a far-fetched idea. And if you're only somewhere for a few months of the year, you want to make sure the landscape really delivers. Especially if you're moving to warmer climates, you don't want to see the bare sticks you'd see at home. With that, I've selected a range of plants that will be at their best in sequence during the winter and early spring months. Manzanita serves as the big backdrop to your winter landscape, with evergreen leaves and white blooms that mimic the snow you're avoiding by moving south. Torch aloe serves as the counterpoint to snow with bright red blooms in winter. Indian hawthorn will follow in early spring with pink blooms on a mid-size hedge. While wall germander blooms in summer, I still include this in a winter home getaway because it can create a beautiful year-round hedge that is incredibly fragrant. Not only does it add some fragrance to your landscape, but you can dry the plant and use it in potpourri. And let's face it, flowers aren't the be-all and end-all. Fragrant leaves definitely make a difference!

RECIPE CARD

REGION Arid or high elevation climate (less than 10 inches / 25 cm of annual rainfall or elevation above 5,000 feet / 1,524 meters)

STYLE Martha: The Classic

GOAL Glamorize a mountain getaway retreat at a high elevation in rocky soil

Living at a high elevation doesn't mean you're only stuck with green shrubs and trees. A great diversity of plant material can survive at high elevation. If you live there or are just visiting, you can be greeted with amazing texture and color. While privet may be invasive in some areas, varieties such as Straight Talk (which produces little to no seed) were discovered in the mountains of Colorado. While not native to the area, the plants have adapted well to the low humidity and high elevation. They serve as a great upright backdrop to the rest of your planting, which can include swaths of purple coneflower, yellow tickseed, and Rocky Mountain columbine. The columbine will bloom first, followed by the tickseed and coneflower, allowing the design to feel intentional and not crowded. Even in the mountains, you can create beauty!

Rocky Mountain columbine (*Aquilegia saximontana*)

Purple coneflower (*Echinacea purpurea*)

Tickseed (*Coreopsis grandiflora*)

Privet (*Ligustrum vulgare*)

KELLY
The Naturalist

From Martha's classic approach, we'll loosen things up a bit with Kelly's more naturalistic style. Like Martha's recipes, I encourage you to spend some time with Kelly's plants, even if you don't feel like this is your exact aesthetic, because you might be inspired by something you see. And again, there are so many plants out there, you just might find your new favorite plant that can also be used in your preferred style. From airy grasses to colorful prairie plants, Kelly's plant palette gives you the broadest range of material that you'll find in the book. Shrubs, trees, grasses, perennials, and more will fill these landscapes.

Replacing a turf lawn with a mix of regionally-appropriate plants can paint a living tapestry with amazing ecological value.

RECIPE CARD

REGION Cold climate (Down to -30°F / -34°C)
STYLE Kelly: The Naturalist
GOAL Celebrate fall

Creating a prairie-like landscape is a fabulous way to build a fall-first garden. These plants leap from the ground and showcase a stunning array of color and texture that make you never want to leave. Using purple love grass creates a low purple haze like cotton candy. Especially from a distance, that frothy texture looks good enough to eat. Rising just above that froth is the complementary color of the orange coneflower with its individual petals and rounded shape, singular vertical purple flower of the prairie blazing star, and finally the red-purple mounded blooms of Joe-pye weed. The purple theme with a splash of orange is striking, as is the combination of shapes that rise from the haze of the ornamental grass. This is a celebration of fall in a naturalistic planting.

Joe-pye weed (*Eutrochium spp.*)

Orange coneflower (*Rudbeckia fulgida*)

Prairie blazing star (*Liatris pycnostachya*)

Purple love grass (*Eragrostis spectabilis*)

Lotus Moon pearlbush (*Exochorda x macrantha* 'Bailmoon')

Snowberry (*Symphoricarpos albus*)

RECIPE CARD

REGION Cold climate (Down to -30°F / -34°C)
STYLE Kelly: The Naturalist
GOAL Establish a full sun garden with sandy soil

Sandy soil isn't a scary thing for Kelly's type of design. As long as it's sandy loam and not straight beach sand, you're doing just fine. Lotus Moon pearlbush is one of my favorite plants to use in a cold climate garden. It's rock-solid hardy and is one of the first shrubs of a decent size to put on a flower show in the spring. The entire plant is covered in little white blooms that create a massive affect. This plant can get some size on it, so plant it near the back of your flower bed, along a fence line, or to create a border. Balance the shrub with the switchgrass on either end to add some summer and fall excitement with the red fronds of the grass. The purple of the ornamental onion plays nicely against the sage-blue leaves of the pearlbush, and the snowberry develops big white berries in fall, repeating the color scheme from spring, but now complemented by the fizzy seed heads of the ornamental grass.

Millennium ornamental onion (*Allium* hybrid)

Shenandoah switchgrass (*Panicum virgatum*)

RECIPE CARD

REGION Temperate climate (Down to -5°F / -21°C)
STYLE Kelly: The Naturalist
GOAL Focus on native plant selections

Planting native or nativar—cultivated selections of native species—is the best place to start when working with this type of design. Remember how I talked about how Kelly chooses plants based on the place in which you're planting? Well, that's the very definition of native plants. They are naturally adapted to survive and thrive, meaning less work and less water to keep them going. While native plants can be somewhat rangy at times, this selection of native species gives you plants with solid structure and fabulous color that draws in pollinators left and right. The blooms start with your stunning pea-shaped blue flowers on your false indigo shortly followed by the sweetspire, which has gorgeous white racemes that cover the plant with caterpillar-like blooms. It's a really impressive way to start off the season, and both plants will stay full and be a beautiful leafy backdrop for summer and fall. The next in your succession of blooms is the bright red of the cardinal flower, which then transitions to the lavender-rose flowers of bee balm. Each of these brings unique shape, texture, color, and pollinators to the landscape, and their native ecological benefits make them even more alluring.

Blue false indigo (*Baptisia australis*)

Love Child sweetspire (*Itea virginica* 'Bailteaone')

Petite delight bee balm (*Monarda didyma*)

Cardinal flower (*Lobelia cardinalis*)

Culver's root (*Veronicastrum virginicum*)

Little Angel burnet (*Sanguisorba officinalis var. microcephala*)

Little Zebra Japanese silver grass (*Miscanthus sinensis*)

RECIPE CARD

REGION **Temperate climate (Down to -5°F / -21°C)**
STYLE **Kelly: The Naturalist**
GOAL **Achieve masses of summer color**

When we talked about scale and pattern in Chapter 4, that's where this comes into play. You can create bulk color with just a few species of plants when you plant en masse. Using the Little Zebra grass as the spine of your design, plant this spotted, finely textured grass in groups, and then start filling in pockets with the other varieties, overlapping some to look like a more natural planting. In this mix, I prefer a white-flowered Culver's root to play with the red flowers of Little Angel burnet and yellow blooms of American Gold Rush. Little Angel is one of my favorites to use in this type of design because of its fluidity and seemingly floating bottlebrush flowers hanging above the planting, not to mention the variegated foliage at its base. These play especially well with the spotted leaves of the silver grass and also have a similar texture to the Culver's root flowers, bringing it all together. I add the black-eyed Susan to this mix to offer that complementary color scheme that adds brightness and to bring a rounded shape to the garden that remains until frost. Choose a selection like American Gold Rush that is highly disease resistant for clean foliage and blooms.

American Gold Rush black-eyed Susan (*Rudbeckia* hybrid)

RECIPE CARD

REGION Subtropic climate (Down to 20°F / -6°C)
STYLE Kelly: The Naturalist
GOAL Create decorative pots that brighten up a shady area

As temperatures rise and sun exposure decreases, we get to be creative in finding fun ways to brighten up the space. BananAppeal is a cultivated native plant in the southeastern United States that is a bright yellow-chartreuse foliage plant that stays bright in a shady place. I love this because it's like bringing a bit of sunshine to an otherwise darker position in the landscape. And doing it in a decorative pot elevates that color off the ground so you've got a little pot of happiness nearer eye level. I like to pair this variety with Purple Heart, which will trail down the front of the decorative pot with its deep purple leaves, giving a fabulous complementary color to the bright chartreuse of BananAppeal. But what fun is one pot if you can have two, right? To add a bit of texture to this colorful shade display, add a second pot in differing size with a spider plant. It'll add texture and movement as the leaves blow in the wind, and it also adds additional shape to the space with its upward and then cascading leaves contrasting with the upright habit of the small anise tree.

BananAppeal small anise tree (*Illicium parviflorum* 'PIIIP-I')

Purple heart (*Setcreasea pallida*)

Spider plant (*Chlorophytum comosun*)

Dwarf morning glory (*Evolvulus glomeratus*)

Flip Side chaste tree (*Vitex x* 'Bailtexone')

Mexican feather grass (*Stipa tenuissima*)

Butterfly weed (*Asclepias tuberosa*)

RECIPE CARD

REGION **Subtropic climate (Down to 20°F / -6°C)**
STYLE **Kelly: The Naturalist**
GOAL **Plant near a sandy beach in full sun**

If you're one of the lucky ones with a beach house in a subtropic climate, please know that I am incredibly jealous of you. And even more so when we talk about what plants you can use in your landscape! One of my favorite plants for this climate that can handle the sandy soil and saltwater breeze is chaste tree. I especially love Flip Side because it's got such unique foliage and stays relatively compact. As the leaves flutter in the wind, you see the dusty olive top of the leaves as well as the purple underside. It's such a cool and unique trait that it deserves a central focus in the garden. Beyond the leaves, the plant is covered in soft spiky purple flowers all summer and fall; if you deadhead the early blooms, you'll get more throughout the growing season. This thing is a pollinator magnet too. Wins all around. The lobed leaves of the chaste tree are especially fun against Mexican feather grass, which only gets about 2 feet (just over a half meter) tall and wide. The soft, feathery plumes build a little carpet underneath the shrub. Mixing butterfly weed in small patches in context with the grass is a great way to add additional color—the orange bloom is fabulous with the blue of the chaste tree—and add pollinator-friendly plants. To finish off this design, we need a groundcover carpet of flowers. Remember that Kelly's aesthetic is about planting with density and not relying on wood mulch or rocks to fill gaps between larger plants. Dwarf morning glory is a perfect way to cap off this design as it spreads across the ground without becoming invasive, and it has analogous color to the chaste tree, finishing off the look with a clean, yet full feeling.

RECIPE CARD

REGION Arid or high elevation climate (Less than 10 inches / 25 cm of annual rainfall or elevation above 5,000 feet / 1,524 meters)

STYLE Kelly: The Naturalist

GOAL Make a rock garden interesting with color and texture

A rock garden is a perfect fit for this collector design style. We love a good challenge and finding combinations of plants that can survive at elevation or with little water is a great way to push boundaries and build out gardens with beautiful, yet sturdy plants. The central focal point of this garden is the Fremont's mahonia, a North American native shrub that checks boxes every season and is drought resistant. It's got yellow flowers, red berries, and blue foliage that remains evergreen throughout the year, and is great as a single plant or to build a shrub hedge. Pretty tough to beat, especially if you like to feed the birds with your garden (those profusion of berries will keep them full). Since the mahonia is the star of the show, we need some backup singers, and in this garden, it will be blanket flower and Indian paintbrush. They have complementary colors, blooming orange and red, with the Indian paintbrush starting earlier in the season, both blooming in summer, and the blanket flower extending into fall. They serve as nice accents to the early yellow flowers on the mahonia and the late-season berries. Finally, we would be remiss if not including a groundcover to fill in some of the gaps between and over the rocks. For this, I love Alpine rock cress with its compact size and white blooms that go with any other color. It looks like a soft snowy blanket below the fiery colors of the perennials above.

Blanket flower (*Gaillardia* spp.)

Fremont's mahonia (*Mahonia fremontii*)

Indian paintbrush (*Castilleja coccinea*)

Alpine rockcress (*Arabis caucasica*)

Large coneflower (*Rudbeckia maxima*)

Pink muhly grass (*Muhlenbergia capillaris*)

Anise hyssop (*Agastache* hybrid)

Mexican daisy (*Erigeron karvinskianus*)

RECIPE CARD

REGION **Arid or high elevation climate (Less than 10 inches / 25 cm of annual rainfall or elevation above 5,000 feet / 1,524 meters)**

STYLE **Kelly: The Naturalist**

GOAL **Minimize supplemental water with a xeriscape planting**

Similar to the rock planting, xeriscape design is focused on drought-tolerant plants, and specifically with the intention of having zero or limited applied water. In a xeriscape design, you move away from a traditional irrigation system and rely on naturally occurring water from rain or underground sources. In this design, we get to use my favorite ornamental grass and one of my favorite plants of all time: pink muhly grass. Maybe it's because it won't survive my winters, but I just think it's so magical, creating a glistening cloud of pink in the garden. Adding to the pink mist is the hyssop, which peeks above the ornamental grass with pollinator-loved orange and lavender blooms perfect for hummingbirds and bees. Rising even further above are the large coneflower, adding some height to the xeriscape with complementary yellow flowers throughout the summer. If you let the coneflower go to seed, you'll even find some birds having a snack later in the season. Along the edge of the xeriscape garden, I suggest adding Mexican daisy, a low-growing, trailing perennial that will creep around rocks or other hard surfaces as it works near the pink muhly grass. It is covered in white flowers that age to pink, which also are loved by pollinators.

TOMMY
The Minimalist

While this design style is focused more on minimal plants for maximum impact, that doesn't mean that there's any lack of personality or flavor in Tommy's approach. We cover all seasons, all climates, and a variety of plant types. This is a fun challenge, to create a chic and clean look with living things that don't always play by the rules. Choosing plants that can be somewhat predictable plays a key role, while balancing that structure with beauty. Similar to Martha's style, this style also focuses on selecting species that are low maintenance yet provide pleasing and specific impact in the landscape. Flip forward to see what Tommy's got to offer.

This small yard is Tommy to the max. Minimalistic, clean, and functional.

Boxwood (*Buxus* spp.)

Tulip (*Tulipa* spp.)

Big bluestem grass (*Andropogon gerardii*)

Smooth hydrangea (*Hydrangea arborescens*)

RECIPE CARD

REGION **Cold climate (Down to -30°F / -34°C)**
STYLE **Tommy: The Minimalist**
GOAL **Ensure four seasons of visual interest**

Creating a four-season garden in a cold climate while appreciating a minimalistic, chic design can be intimidating. But using the right mix of plants makes it easy and enjoyable. Let's start with structure. Where do you want to create the line of sight in this space? Use the boxwood to establish the foundational piece of your design. This is likely a straight line, square, or L shape to keep it clean and crisp. This will help you plan everything else in this garden. Next, I would plant the smooth hydrangea, as this shrub will be your summer and early fall focal point. Depending on the variety, you'll get big round blooms of white or pink. Lining a driveway? Plant boxwood in front with a hedge of hydrangea in back. Creating a more formal entryway? Follow the classic English-style garden and create a box on each side of the walkway and fill the box with hydrangea, remembering to keep mature size in mind. Behind the hydrangea, or at the back end of the box, plant big bluestem grass, which will add fall interest to the design, while keeping those clean lines. Big bluestem is an upright grass that adds architectural value to the landscape and is a star in the fall garden as the hydrangea blooms fade. A final thing to plant is white tulip bulbs, which will pop up in spring to fill in behind the boxwood and bloom before the hydrangeas begin to grow and leaf out in late spring. This way you have all four seasons covered and you still keep a refined, modern look.

RECIPE CARD

REGION Cold climate (Down to -30°F / -34°C)
STYLE Tommy: The Minimalist
GOAL Beautify a summer lake home

If you're in a cooler climate like me, getting away to a lake home or cabin is the perfect way to spend a summer weekend. And having a beautifully landscaped getaway is even more idyllic. When designing, I like to start big and work to the smaller plants. Start with what's going to frame the garden and take up the most space, and then work down to the details. A columnar birch tree is a great way to set sight lines and build context around your lake home garden. The height is an anchor, and a columnar form keeps the rigidity of clean lines present. In the flower bed for a minimalistic aesthetic, keep to fewer species and let each one shine. In this design, I would plant Fireside ninebark in back, followed by Little Hottie hydrangea, and then a compact shrubby cinquefoil (*Potentilla fruticosa*). These specific varieties work so well together because the ninebark has incredibly dark purple, almost black leaves, and are a fabulous backdrop to the clean white blooms of Little Hottie, which is shorter than the ninebark and would make a lovely hedge. A compact potentilla in front rounds out the design by maintaining a small ball-shaped shrub that is easy to maintain and adds additional summer and fall color to the landscape without making it look messy or overgrown. Clean lines, chic colors, and structural framing make this a perfect cold-hardy lake home design.

Columnar birch tree (*Betula platyphylla*)

Little Hottie panicle hydrangea (*Hydrangea paniculata* 'Bailpanone')

Fireside ninebark (*Physocarpus opulifolius* 'UMNHarpell')

Shrubby cinquefoil (*Potentilla fruticosa*)

Straight & Narrow Japanese holly (*Ilex crenata* 'PIIIC-I')

Cotoneaster (*Cotoneaster spp.*)

Sweet alyssum (*Lobularia maritima*)

Cobalt-n-Gold hypericum (*Hypericum kalmianum* 'PIIHYP-I')

RECIPE CARD

REGION **Temperate climate (Down to -5°F / -21°C)**
STYLE **Tommy: The Minimalist**
GOAL **Fill a sunny coastal landscape with structure and refined color**

Moving from the lake home to the temperate coast, our design approach remains similar. Upright framing, tightly shaped shrubs and hedges, and a low-growing plant in front to serve as a classy accent. In this warmer climate, Straight & Narrow Japanese holly is a go-to plant. There are other upright hollies on the market, but they tend to splay over time and detract from the clean look this aesthetic demands. Straight & Narrow keeps a perfectly tight form so your evergreen column stands tall in the garden. The other structural plants in this design are cotoneaster, which makes a lovely hedge with spring blooms and late summer and fall berries, and Cobalt-n-Gold hypericum. I call out this specific variety of hypericum for a couple of reasons. It's not the type of hypericum you might think of for cut arrangements with berries. Instead, it's got fine leaves that are blue-green in color and a mass of yellow flowers in summer. It's also super clean in terms of its mounded shape. You don't need to shear it; the plant just stays round and gorgeous with the lovely texture of the foliage. As the mat in front, I love the idea of using sweet alyssum, which adds flower power in spring and again in fall. The blooms may fade a bit in the summer heat, but that's okay because you've got the hypericum going at full bore.

RECIPE CARD

REGION Temperate climate (Down to -5°F / -21°C)
STYLE Tommy: The Minimalist
GOAL Build beautiful decorative containers

With Tommy's design style, planting containers to add color and texture to a modern landscape can be pretty simple and straight forward. We don't want to overdo it, or it won't match the surroundings. For this, I'm making two simple recommendations with only one plant species per container. You could do a big pot with multiples of each variety, but don't mix and match. Hydrangeas are gorgeous in the ground, and the compact varieties are equally as beautiful in decorative pots. I like to use BloomStruck hydrangea because it is naturally smaller, has cool red stems that you can see a bit more when in a pot, and re-blooms with blue-purple or dark pink flowers (depending on your soil pH). The hydrangea alone in the pot is enough in this style. It's classy, elegant, and beautiful all by itself. If you'd like to add a little bit more to the look, find a smaller or shorter pot and plant blue oat grass. The slate blue color plays well with the blue-purple or pink flowers of BloomStruck, fills a decorative pot nicely with its fine and structural leaves, and cascades slightly to give some movement to the overall look. Clean and simple—no need to go overboard with this design.

BloomStruck hydrangea (*Hydrangea macrophylla* 'PIIHM-II')

Blue oat grass (*Helictotrichon sempervirens*)

Sweet woodruff (*Galium odoratum*)

Japanese cedar (*Cryptomeria japonica*)

Swing Low distylium (*Distylium* 'PIIDIST-VI')

Snowbush (*Breynia disticha*)

RECIPE CARD

REGION Subtropic climate (Down to 20°F / -6°C)
STYLE Tommy: The Minimalist
GOAL Provide structure in a partially shaded courtyard

In warmer climates, shade can be a blessing for plants in the mid-summer heat. Especially with this design style, a combination of flowers and foliage in partially shaded areas can be incredibly beautiful. Let's start with structure. Japanese cedar is an evergreen tree in the conifer family that has really interesting texture and serves as a great neutral backdrop or as a pillar on the corner of your home or flower bed. Depending on the variety, they can get over 50 feet (15 meters) or, like Chapel View Japanese cedar, stay fairly compact at under 10 feet (3 meters). To keep the structural theme, I love using snowbush as a small hedge with personality. It only gets 2 to 4 feet (0.6 to 1.2 meters) tall, and the leaves are white and green with red coloring. It's still a nice way to keep structure while adding a little pizzazz for some personality. As you get lower to the ground, distylium is a newer evergreen species to the home landscape that has become really popular because it's so disease resistant. Swing Low matures to only 2 to 3 feet (0.6 to 1 meter), so it adds a level just under the snowbush with a lovely dark green that mirrors the Japanese cedar. As you work down to the ground level, adding sweet woodruff brings a carpet of white blooms in late spring and summer and then leaves vanilla-scented fragrance through fall. A nice balance of color without going overboard, plus structural elements that fit the bill perfectly.

RECIPE CARD

REGION Subtropic climate (Down to 20°F / -6°C)
STYLE Tommy: The Minimalist
GOAL Add color against a newly constructed modern home

Moving into a new home is an epic moment in life. Especially a sleek new house that you get to add a little va-va-voom to with plants! In this design, we'll add some seasonal flower color, fancy foliage, and a decorative pot with a familiar, structural flower. Lunar Magic is one of my favorite crape myrtle because it's more compact than many of the traditional varieties, making it a perfect fit for a new construction landscape. The dark leaves and crisp white flowers make it really stand out, but not in an ostentatious way. It's a disease-resistant variety, so the dark leaves will stay that way until it loses its leaves in late fall, and the white flowers are such a nice contrast. Crimson Fire is a compact variety of the warm-climate standard plant, the fringe flower. This plant keeps its dark red leaves year-round, gives you zig-zag pink flowers in late winter, and keeps a compact mounded shape that is especially impactful in groups (remember the Fibonacci numbers). The final in-ground plant I recommend is garden croton. This baby has such cool, multi-colored foliage that looks like spray-painted leaves that arise from the garden. The final step to this design is adding bird of paradise into decorative pots to frame your front door, a walkway, or staircase. These plants put out blooms year-round, the flowers perched atop long, sturdy stems. It's a great accent to the flower and foliage show in back.

Garden croton (*Codiaeum variegatum*)

Lunar Magic crape myrtle (*Lagerstroemia* 'Baillagone')

Crimson Fire fringe flower (*Loropetalum chinense var. rubrum* 'PIILC-I')

Bird of paradise (*Strelitzia reginae*)

Adam's needle yucca (*Yucca filamentosa*)

Bunny ears cactus (*Opuntia microdasys*)

Agave (*Agave* spp.)

Hens and chicks (*Sempervivum spp.*)

RECIPE CARD

REGION	Arid or high elevation climate (Less than 10 inches / 25 cm of annual rainfall or elevation above 5,000 feet / 1,524 meters)
STYLE	Tommy: The Minimalist
GOAL	Focus on succulents for a chic design

Succulents are the perfect fit for an arid garden. They literally are biologically adapted to retain water and survive in climates that don't have consistent water sources. Esthetically, they're also spot-on for Tommy's design style with their clean, obvious shapes. This recipe can be mixed and matched, depending on the layout of your space. Admittedly, agave is a broad option to suggest, but I want you to choose based on the space you've got to work with. They offer fabulous upward movement, keeping the visitor's eye moving through the space. Adam's needle is another favorite because of its spiky leaves that shoot out of the garden. They also have a bonus moment in summer when a protrusion of white blooms jump from the center of the plant. Without the blooms, it's a really cool plant. With the blooms, it's spectacular. Bunny ears cactus is too cute to not include. It's a more compact variety that creates structural mounds about 2 to 3 feet (0.6 to 1 meter) above the ground, creating a mogul-like affect that add motion to the landscape. Finally, in places where you've got openings and want to add a short burst of color, hens and chicks are the cutest little succulents that can be planted in small groups or as a mat. They are especially useful in decorative pots, in the open crevasse of a wall, or at the base of another upward-facing plant to serve as a visual launching pad.

RECIPE CARD

REGION Arid or high elevation climate (Less than 10 inches / 25 cm of annual rainfall or elevation above 5,000 feet / 1,524 meters)

STYLE Tommy: The Minimalist

GOAL Utilize ornamental grasses for a clean look

Along the same lines as our succulent love on the last page, ornamental grasses are also great ways to add beauty to an arid garden with a clean, modern look. With this recipe, I'm not necessarily recommending they all go together, based on space, but pick and choose what you love. Pampas grass is one of my favorites to yearn for as a cold-climate gardener. The huge plumes that bust from the stems are what Pinterest dreams are made of. And when I was wedding planning, they were on everyone's wedding board. The strong, architectural stems and poofs on top are delicious. Zebra grass is an upright vase-shaped grass that is great on its own or in the background of a hedge planting so that the gradual arch is all that shows. I love this grass because each stem is striped like divider lanes painted on the road. A little highlighter every inch or so. Slight color variation to add a little interest to an otherwise sleek grass. Blue fescue is a low-growing, clumping, blue grass that stays at 1 foot (0.3 meters) high or less. This is great in a border, or you can plant it en masse to fill a larger area in a monoculture, meaning just one species of plant. Finally, one of my other favorites that makes me green with envy is Japanese blood grass. Nice name, right? It gets that moniker from the deep red color the foliage turns in fall. This grass is similar size to the fescue, so planting en masse or in lines throughout the garden gives a perfect paint swath of red throughout your design. It's stunning. So, pick and choose your favorites and what fits the scale of your space.

Pampas grass (*Cortaderia selloana*)

Japanese blood grass (*Imperata cylindrica*)

Zebra grass (*Miscanthus sinensis* 'Zebrinus')

Blue fescue (*Festuca glauca*)

More Plant Choices for Each Garden Style

Now that you've got the tools to design your outdoor space and a starting point for plant selection with the recipes from this chapter, it's time to get out and make it happen. But before I send you on your own, I wanted to give a few more plant ideas based on which persona best fits your aesthetic. This book is all about setting you up for success to make the right plant decisions for your outdoor space, climate, and style. And now you know how to make planting decisions for yourself, but I'm here to help with a few more ideas.

I've created a few charts to add to your plant hunting list based on Kelly, Tommy, and Martha's styles. Each chart drives more plant specifics with notes on climate and what characteristics make them worthy of consideration for your home space. There are hundreds of additional plants to choose from, but these are some of the most readily available plants that you'll find at garden centers or online to fit your aesthetic. Happy shopping!

MORE PLANT CHOICES FOR A MARTHA GARDEN

COMMON & BOTANICAL NAME	CATEGORY	CLIMATE	CHARACTERISTICS
Pagoda dogwood *Cornus alternifolia*	Small tree	Cold to temperate	Pagoda dogwood is a fabulous small tree with layered, horizontal branching that gives a sense of elegance to the garden. It's a fabulous four-season tree with spring flowers, summer berries, and fabulous burgundy fall color, and the branches catch snow in fall, giving a layer cake look to the garden.
Crabapple *Malus* spp.	Tree	Cold to temperate	Saying crabapple is opening a big can of worms because, oh boy, are there a lot of species and cultivars available! But that's why I recommend it for your Martha-inspired garden. They're a superstar of the early-season landscape, are adorned with berries in late summer and fall, and have a great mix of shapes and sizes that can fill the space you've got available.
Ginkgo *Ginkgo biloba*	Tree	Cold to subtropic	The fan-shaped leaves of the ginkgo tree are one of my favorites. It adds such majesty to the garden, and if you've got space to fill, this multi-season wonder is one of my favorites. It's incredibly adaptable to soil types, does well in urban environments, and serves as a great shade tree. This is one of the oldest living species of plants on the planet and pre-dates dinosaurs.
Peach *Prunus persica*	Tree	Temperate to subtropic	This type of garden yearns for a small fruit tree, and peaches are one of my favorites. The blooms are a showstopper in spring followed by fruit in summer. As an added bonus, peaches are easy to grow at home!
Star magnolia *Magnolia stellata*	Small tree	Cold to temperate	Especially in cooler climates, we ache for some color in the landscape after a long winter. Star magnolias are one of the earlier bloomers, and as a large shrub or small tree, they have big impact in the early-season garden as the wavy flowers start to unfold.

→

COMMON & BOTANICAL NAME	CATEGORY	CLIMATE	CHARACTERISTICS
Seven-son flower *Heptacodium miconioides*	Small tree/large shrub	Cold to subtropic	A lesser known but incredibly deserving species, seven-son flower is another one of those that just keeps giving. Exfoliating bark in winter, white flowers in late summer as the monarchs migrate, and unique red flower brachts in fall make this a focal point in a pollinator-friendly garden. New varieties such as Tianshan bring the overall size down so it fits better in most landscapes.
Smokebush *Cotinus coggygria*	Shrub	Temperate	Beautiful lobed leaves are surpassed only by the most unusual flowers that appear as a cloud of smoke, consuming the plant in a stunning display in summer. This is one of those plants people will ask you about at an outdoor dinner party.
Hydrangea *Hydrangea* spp.	Shrub	Cold to temperate	There's no more classic plant than a hydrangea. There are a number of common species at the garden center, and most will fit well with Martha's style. Bigleaf, smooth, and panicle hydrangeas will serve you best based on your climate, sun exposure, and color palette.
Rose *Rosa* spp.	Shrub	Cold to subtropic	To contradict my previous statement, roses are arguably one of the most common shrubs, especially in a cottage-style garden. The never-ending blooms, cut flower possibilities, and fragrance are a landscape staple. Collections like the Easy Elegance series take the hassle out of antique roses and make them super easy to grow.
Spirea *Spiraea* spp.	Shrub	Cold to temperate	Spirea is another one of those staple-plants-for-a-reason. You may see them everywhere, especially in cool-climate gardens, but that's because they just work. They're easy to maintain, give seasons-long color, and bloom their faces off. To me, there's nothing wrong with a little bit of reliable color in the garden.
Chaste tree *Vitex agnus-castus*	Shrub	Temperate to subtropic	While the leaves of the chaste tree may look like another, sometimes illegal green substance when it's not in flower, they add great texture to the garden. And when this thing blooms, it blooms like crazy with cone-like blooms that are major pollinator attractants. Newer varieties bring the size down to a more manageable shrub and can rebloom if deadheaded. My new favorite is Flip Side chaste tree because its leaves are olive colored on top and purple on the bottom, so as they flicker in the wind, you get so much added color to the garden.
Lilac *Syringa* spp.	Shrub	Cold to temperate	Remember how I said that Martha's style is classic? Well, it doesn't get much more classic and beloved than the fragrant, spring-blooming lilac in cooler climates. There has been a massive amount of breeding work done with lilacs, so you have different colors, sizes, and shapes to fit whatever space you've got available. Some varieties even rebloom so you get more lilac flowers later in summer!
Japanese snow-ball viburnum *Viburnum plicatum*	Shrub	Temperate to subtropic	I love this species of viburnum because it just gives and gives and gives, and that's what Martha expects. Snowball-like blooms reminiscent of hydrangeas emerge in spring, the corrugated green leaves add texture in summer, and the fall color is just spectacular.
Russian sage *Perovskia atriplicifolia*	Perennial	Cold to subtropic	If you're looking for a long summer-blooming perennial that doesn't have any major issues, Russian sage is a solid go-to. Its purple blooms last summer into fall on upright stems. They're great pollinator plants and are beautiful by themselves or in a group, especially popping up throughout a colorful flower bed. The leaves are fragrant when crushed, so pull a few off at your next party and show off a little bit!

COMMON & BOTANICAL NAME	CATEGORY	CLIMATE	CHARACTERISTICS
Phlox *Phlox paniculata*	Perennial	Cold to temperate	Another fantastic perennial bloomer that gives you long-lasting color is the fragrant phlox. They come in a wide array of colors, some soft and gentle while some are bright and bold. Their rounded cone-like flowers pop up in the garden for that great summer and fall color, and they can be mixed and matched for some variation and to add personality. Some phlox can be affected by powdery mildew, so I especially like the Candy Store series that includes Bubblegum Pink, Cotton Candy, and Grape Lollipop.
Peony *Paeonia lactiflora*	Perennial	Cold to temperate	Bringing us back to nostalgia and classics, it's tough to beat peonies in the spring. The ruffled, sumptuous blooms are a great transition from spring to summer and are fabulous as cut flowers to brighten up your day. Pro tip: Ants love peonies, so be sure to plant them away from your doorway.
Catmint *Nepeta* spp.	Perennial	Cold to temperate	You may look at catmint and think that it looks like Russian sage, and you wouldn't be wrong. Both are upright shoots of purple flowers. Where it differs is that catmint has more natural fragrance, the spikes of flowers are held tighter and appear more dense, and you'll see blooms earlier in the season. Both are excellent perennials for your garden, so pick and choose based on bloom time, aesthetic, size, and shape that you need to fill out your plan.
Maiden grass *Miscanthus* spp.	Perennial	Cold to subtropic	One of the most recognizable ornamental grasses, maiden grass is beloved for Martha's aesthetic because it gives a multi-dimensional, textured, flowy backdrop to the landscape. With thin, arching leaves, plumes of feathery grassy blooms in late summer and fall, and fabulous late season foliage color, there's a reason it is so popular. There are a wide range of species and varieties available so you can find one for most landscapes and decorative containers.
Bleeding heart *Lamprocapnos spectabilis*	Perennial	Cold to subtropic	Finding beautiful plants for shade, especially in spring, can be tough. But bleeding hearts are a solid choice for that exact scenario. The long stems of heart-shaped pink, red, or white blooms draping off give such brightness and beauty as your shade garden starts to wake up. They're adaptable to most soils, are rabbit resistant, and don't have major disease issues.
Lavender *Lavandula* spp.	Perennial	Temperate to subtropic	We all know lavender for its calming properties in candles, lotions, oils, and more, but it's also a dreamy garden perennial. Growing in mounds of (usually) purple fragrant flowers, lavender does best in warm conditions with dry soil. If you get too much water, try lavender in containers so you can still enjoy the fragrance and flowers up close throughout the season.
Clematis *Clematis* spp.	Perennial vine	Cold to subtropic	Clematis vines bring a tropical flavor to the landscape, winding themselves up a lattice, trellis, or thin rod. They wrap their leaves around the support structure, so thin is good in this instance. There are different types of clematis that bloom at different times of year, so do a little research to be sure you buy the right one, and then go fill your open spaces with clematis color.

MORE PLANT CHOICES FOR A TOMMY GARDEN

COMMON & BOTANICAL NAME	CATEGORY	CLIMATE	CHARACTERISTICS
Parkland Pillar Birch *Betula platyphylla*	Upright tree	Cold to temperate	This specific variety is a perfect combination of nature and structure. Parkland Pillar gives the rigid upright structure you'd expect from Tommy's aesthetic, but gives you a nod to nature with the classic birch bark at the base. Fall color on this beauty is spectacular in cold and temperate climates.
Japanese maple *Acer palmatum*	Tree	Temperate	Known for their fabulous color with sharply lobed leaves, Japanese maple trees bring a level of refinement to the garden that is tough to beat. While they do bloom and develop seed heads, the most prominent feature is the incredible leaf color throughout the season—especially in fall—and the structure from the trunk, branches, and leaves themselves.
Hornbeam *Carpinus* spp.	Tree	Cold to subtropic	Hornbeam are fantastic trees to be pleached, forming structured allées and elevated structure. This is perfectly in line with Tommy's aesthetic, using live plants to add structure to the outdoor space. I mean, if you can create a living wall instead of just using paint, why wouldn't you?
Crape myrtle *Lagerstroemia* spp.	Small tree/large shrub	Temperate to subtropic	A staple in warmer climates, crape myrtle can be grown as trees or large shrubs, depending on the variety. They boast incredible texture, variation in leaf and bloom color, and have a striking presence. Many of the newer varieties are especially strong rebloomers, if deadheaded, putting out new blooms every 5–6 weeks until fall.
Arborvitae *Thuja* spp.	Small tree/large shrub	Cold to temperate	It's tough to beat the structure and lines that arborvitae bring to a cold-climate landscape. There are a multitude of varieties in different sizes and shapes, but the evergreen, textured foliage provides year-round support (and a great green backdrop to a snowy landscape).
Frangipani *Plumeria* spp.	Small tree/large shrub	Subtropic to tropic	My major zone envy kicks in here! Frangipani are the tree whose flowers make up the classic Hawaiian lei, and you can have it in your yard (if your winter temperatures stay above 50 degrees Fahrenheit [10 degrees Celsius]). Incredibly fragrant and colorful, this brings the tropics to your landscape. I especially love these for Tommy's style because they grow upright with branches that turn at sharp angles, bringing a more linear shape to the structural parts of the tree, and then have a beautifully round canopy.
Straight & Narrow Japanese holly *Ilex crenata*	Shrub	Temperate to subtropic	Incredible strong branches hold this variety tall and tight, giving you rigid cylindrical shape to the landscape. Other varieties tend to splay out as they age, distracting from the intended clean lines.
Distylium *Distylium* spp.	Shrub	Temperate to subtropic	Many think of boxwood as the classic structural evergreen for a modern garden, but there's a new evergreen in town! Distylium are super disease resistant, come in a variety of shapes and sizes, and bring a fantastic structural element to your border or flower bed.

COMMON & BOTANICAL NAME	CATEGORY	CLIMATE	CHARACTERISTICS
Weigela *Weigela* spp.	Shrub	Cold to temperate	I love weigela for Tommy's aesthetic because it's incredibly easy to manage (plant it and forget it) and can bring great blocks of color and shape to the garden without all the hassle. Newer varieties can keep a refined short hedge without pruning and have the bonus of trumpet-like flowers in early summer. I especially love Shining Sensation because of its incredibly dark purple leaves that don't bleach in full sun, which are accented by bright pink flowers.
Yew *Taxus* spp.	Shrub	Cold to subtropic	Another evergreen shrub (or small tree depending on the species), yews have more needle-like leaves than arborvitae but can be shaped into fantastic hedges with extended heat tolerance. Many yew can be clipped into hedges while other species are more upright and columnar.
Big-leaf paper plant *Fatsia japonica*	Shrub	Subtropic to tropic	The large lobed leaves gladly fill space with real wow factor. The sharp shape of the leaves makes it a great fit for Tommy's style and are especially enticing as a foundation planting as a pseudo hedge or as a specimen plant in the landscape or container.
Mediterranean spurge *Euphorbia characias*	Shrub	Temperate to subtropic	Narrow blue-green, spiky leaves sit at the base of each upright stem topped with chartreuse flowers in spring that resemble a bottlebrush. As the name suggests, these are great plants for rock gardens and don't require much water. That drought tolerance, plus its resistance to deer and rabbits, make it an easy garden plant that adds fantastic color and unique shape to the landscape.
Alpine currant *Ribes alpinum*	Shrub	Cold to temperate	Alpine currant shrubs naturally grow into an upright hedge shape and can be trimmed into a tight hedge for solid structure. As a bonus, it produces bright red berries late in the season that serve as a fall and winter snack for birds.
Silver mound *Artemisia schmidtiana*	Perennial	Cold to temperate	With fine silver foliage and a perfectly mounded habit, silver mound allows for repetitive humps in the garden with leaves that pair well with most other colors in the garden.
Black mondo grass *Ophiopogon planiscapus*	Perennial	Temperate to subtropic	A fantastic groundcover, this ornamental grass has beautiful arching, almost black leaves. It's a great way to add drama to the landscape when planted as a group. Light pink flowers emerge in summer, beautifully accenting the dark foliage, and then develops purple berries.
Red hot poker *Kniphofia* spp.	Perennial	Temperate to subtropic	Another one of my favorite plants that I can't grow, red hot pokers shoot red, orange, or yellow daggers straight up from the ground, bringing the drama to your landscape. Even with Tommy's more refined aesthetic, these are a fantastic fit with their tight texture and mass of impactful color, each bloom on a single stem.
New Zealand flax *Phormium tenax*	Perennial	Subtropic to tropic	With agave-looking foliage, this evergreen perennial adds sword-like leaves shooting up from the ground. There are green- and purple-leaf varieties available. This perennial can get pretty large, especially in warmer climates, so I love this to line a long driveway, near the back of a garden bed, or as the focal point emerging from a group of low-growing or groundcover plants.

→

COMMON & BOTANICAL NAME	CATEGORY	CLIMATE	CHARACTERISTICS
Lily turf *Liriope muscari*	Perennial	Temperate to tropic	Fantastic in linear rows and impressive en masse, lily turf are clump-forming perennials that are especially impressive in late summer when the purple blooms rise above the arching leaves like spikes. Only growing up to 2 feet (61 cm), these low-growing perennials are beautiful when planted in a group, especially as an understory to trees.
Fountain grass *Pennisetum* spp.	Perennial	Temperate to subtropic	In containers or lining a pathway or driveway, fountain grass adds movement and texture in a way that stays refined for Tommy's aesthetic. This adaptable plant can be used across any design style. The soft bottlebrush plumes emerge in summer.
Butterfly weed *Asclepias* spp.	Perennial	Cold to subtropic	In a modern design, butterfly weed can be planted in groups to bring a wave of bright orange flavor to complement the generally subtle colors of contemporary design. As a bonus, the seed heads in fall have a great upright, dagger-like shape that spring out of the landscape.
Blazing star *Liatrus* spp.	Perennial	Cold to temperate	I love blazing star in a contemporary design because of the fantastic upward structure of this perennial. It allows you to bring some color to your outdoor space without sacrificing clean lines, contrasting compact mounded perennials or shrubs below.
Lily of the Nile *Agapanthus* spp.	Perennial	Temperate to subtropic	Spiky leaves give a great foundation to the starburst blooms protruding straight above the grassy clump. Planting Lily of the Nile in a row along a path gives the repetition that fits Tommy's aesthetic, especially with the sharp lines of all pieces of the plant.
Sedge grass *Carex* spp.	Perennial	Cold to subtropic	This wide-ranging species has a number of uses in the landscape, many of which involve creating a groundcover or serving as structural turf replacement. While some varieties tend toward Kelly's style, many retain clean lines and gracefully arching leaves that allow you to fill a space without relying on mulch or rock, line the pathway to your home or outdoor patio, or are great as specimen plants in small decorative pots.

MORE PLANT CHOICES FOR A KELLY GARDEN

COMMON & BOTANICAL NAME	CATEGORY	CLIMATE	CHARACTERISTICS
Ironwood *Ostrya* spp.	Tree	Cold to temperate	If you've got some space, an ironwood tree is a fantastic addition with textured bark, great fall color, spring catkins, and cute hops-like fruit that appears in late summer.
Japanese stewartia *Stewartia pseudocamellia*	Tree	Temperate	Stewartia is a fabulous small tree for this garden style, with multicolored, decorative bark, arching branches, gorgeous saucer-like white blooms in early summer and incredible fall color. That multi-season interest with added texture and color makes it a Kelly favorite.
Serviceberry *Amelanchier* spp.	Small tree/ large shrub	Cold to temperate	Speaking of multi-season interest, serviceberry is one of those rock star plants that checks all the boxes for Kelly's natural, hard-working style. Spring blooms, summer berries, fall color, and incredible architecture make this a fan favorite.
Witch hazel *Hamamelis* spp.	Small tree/ large shrub	Cold to temperate	Known for the winter or early, early spring blooms that look almost like crooked spider legs (but pretty), witch hazel are fantastic shrubs to add color and texture to the off-peak season in the garden.
Cutleaf sumac *Rhus typhina*	Shrub	Cold to temperate	With the textured cutleaf foliage, this multi-season beauty adds so much texture to the landscape. Especially with the cultivar Tiger Eyes, you'll get green or chartreuse foliage in summer, bright red and orange leaves in fall, and exposed structural staghorn stems in winter.
Sand cherry *Prunus pumila*	Shrub	Cold to temperate	Fabulous as a shrub that can take up some space, this species adds gorgeous lobed leaves and spring flowers to generally challenging locations. Sand cherry do well in rocky and sandy soils. New varieties like Jade Parade are more prostrate, with almost antler-like stems creeping near the ground.
Dogwood *Cornus* spp.	Shrub	Cold to temperate	Dogwood is a broad category, but there are so many species that add to the landscape. They're fantastic structural shrubs for the bulk of the season, but many also bring fire-red stems to the winter garden, spring flowers, and summer berries. Dogwoods are also great for those wet areas in your landscape that drown other plants.
Buttonbush *Cephalanthus occidentalis*	Shrub	Cold to subtropic	Buttonbushes are another species that do extremely well in wet areas of the landscape. Buttonbush has a nice textured leaf, but it is most exciting because of its unique flower that looks like a pincushion. It's also a great pollinator plant and the seed head is food for waterfowl..
Kalm St. John's wort *Hypericum kalmianum*	Shrub	Cold to temperate	This species of St. John's wort isn't probably what you're thinking with the berries that you find in a cut flower arrangement. Kalm St. John's wort has more finely textured leaves, bright yellow flowers, and great fall color. A favorite cultivar is Cobalt-n-Gold because of its slate blue leaves and consistently strong performance.

→

COMMON & BOTANICAL NAME	CATEGORY	CLIMATE	CHARACTERISTICS
Sageleaf willow *Salix candida*	Shrub	Cold to temperate	This species of willow is more cold hardy and generally stays more compact, a perfect fit for the modern landscape. The texture of the leaves is spectacular, and the bonus of the classic willow catkin in early spring is a gorgeous addition. Cultivar Iceberg Alley is a favorite because of its fuzzy silver foliage.
Chokeberry *Aronia* spp.	Shrub	Cold to temperate	Spring through fall, chokeberry is an adaptable, multi-use shrub that is beautiful as a standalone planting or in a hedge. Spring flowers are followed by edible berries in summer, with fiery foliage in fall.
Snowberry/ coralberry *Symphoricarpos* spp.	Shrub	Cold to temperate	An adaptable plant for sun or part shade, snowberry and coralberry shrubs are most loved for their colorful berries in fall. I especially love to plant them along the edge of a woodland to create a bridge between nature and a more loosely designed garden space.
Black-eyed Susan *Rudbeckia* spp.	Perennial	Cold to subtropic	A classic prairie plant, black-eyed Susan are fantastic summer and fall-blooming perennials. They can self-seed, so can fill pockets in the landscape with gorgeous yellow and yellow-orange blooms.
Sneezeweed *Helenium* spp.	Perennial	Cold to temperate	Sneezeweeds are fantastic for adding bright shocks of color in the late part of the season. They naturally grow in more moist areas in the landscape, a solution for a usually troublesome area. The blooms are also fantastic for pollinators!
Coneflower *Echinacea* spp.	Perennial	Cold to temperate	A standard across many design styles, coneflower is included in so many designs for good cause. They are incredibly easy to grow, can handle drought and heat, and add massive swaths of color to the garden. With Kelly's approach, coneflower tend to be planted en masse and can be single color or a mix to have a more natural appeal.
Blue grama grass *Bouteloua gracilis*	Perennial	Cold to subtropic	This is one of my favorite ornamental grasses for Kelly's design style. It's a low-growing, textured grass with a switch-like seed head on the top. Kelly's approach supports removing turf lawns and replacing with native or nativar species, and blue grama grass is used in this exact scenario as it only grows to roughly 1 foot (30 cm).
Cardinal flower *Lobelia cardinalis*	Perennial	Cold to subtropic	A beacon of bright red color in the late summer and early fall garden, cardinal flower shines brightly on spikes that shoot up from clumping foliage. Cardinal flowers are great in areas where soil stays slightly wet and attract hummingbirds and butterflies to the landscape.
Ornamental onion *Allium* spp.	Perennial	Cold to subtropic	You may recognize small purple, round blooms that pop up in many gardens in summer and fall that have chive-like foliage. Well, that is ornamental onion (hence the foliage appearance). There are different species that add additional shapes to the garden, but the reason I love even the most common varieties like Millennium is that the species adds texture and movement from afar and up close.

COMMON & BOTANICAL NAME	**CATEGORY**	**CLIMATE**	**CHARACTERISTICS**
Bladder campion *Silene vulgaris*	Perennial	Cold to temperate	Kelly's style is all about creating moments of surprise and introducing people to new and unique plants. Bladder campion is not something you'd see in a standard landscape, so that's why I love it here. Stems rise from the clumping base and have drooping flowers with five petals surrounding a textured lobe.
Aster *Symphyotrichums* spp. / *Aster* spp.	Perennial	Cold to subtropic	Fall is a fabulous time in the natural, textured garden. Asters are a key component to making this happen. While there are a number of different species, each adds color and texture (see the pattern?) that make the fall garden so special. I also love many of these varieties because they add blue and purple cool tones to the fall garden that is usually full of warm colors.
Joe-pye weed *Eutrochium* spp.	Perennial	Cold to subtropic	Speaking of the fall garden, Joe-pye weed is another classic. Though the name may make you cringe a bit, it's so much more beautiful and functional than a weed. Usually with pink, purple, or red flower heads, Joe-pye weed appear later in the season, growing up from the summer landscape to attract late season pollinators and close out the year on a strong foot.

The Finish Line

Take a deep breath. I know that there were a ton of plants shown in the preceding pages. Not all of them will work for you, but I do hope that you read through everything to see what piqued your interest so you can head to the garden center and do some shopping. Remember that this is just a starting point. There are hundreds of species that will fit your style and climate, so keep digging. Get and stay curious. I've got a ton of other plant selection ideas on Instagram @RyanPlantsPlants, so head over there any time. I'll keep things updated with new varieties, too. Trying new plants is always a fun way to stay engaged, and I'll be your guide for the best of the new.

Building a landscape doesn't have to be a set it and forget it experience. It's a living space that you get to play with and adapt over time. See what you love and what you want to swap out for something new. Don't be scared to kill plants. It happens, and it is just an opportunity to try something different. The most seasoned of gardeners have plants that die for one reason or another. Now that you're on this journey, have conversations. With friends, family, and other people who are digging in the dirt with you. There are a ton of online communities where you can connect with people, ask questions, and find more inspiration. And always feel free to connect with me on Instagram @RyanPlantsPlants. I can't wait to share photos and talk shop with you. So, go. Create beauty, dig in the dirt, and play.

And most of all, have fun.

For More Inspiration

I truly hope that you enjoyed reading the *Field Guild to Outside Style*. While I wish I could cover everything about garden design, that's just not possible in one book. That's why I am so excited to share some of my favorite garden and design books with you. I'm grateful to give you an introduction to digging in the dirt and, depending on where you felt most inspired, offer ideas for your next book purchase or digital deep dive to keep this gardening journey going.

As I've mentioned a few times, garden design isn't just about flowers. And my friends Karen Chapman and Christina Salwitz talk about just that in their book *Fine Foliage*. They give practical and inspiring advice for designing garden spaces and decorative containers with plants using foliage first. They still include flowers, but only if they accent already amazing leaves.

If you fit into the Kelly profile, loving the more natural look, *New Naturalism* by Kelly Norris is a must. He's the inspiration behind the natural aesthetic in this book, so it's a perfect next step for those of you who want to build that dense but loose, cultivated space with interesting plant varieties. Kelly's a brilliant writer; each word pulls you through the text and leaves you with so many useable ideas and plant selections.

Another book in the natural realm is *Planting in a Post-Wild World* by Claudia West and Thomas Rainer. They catapult the idea of combining the wild world of native planting with the more cultivated space of a modern garden. Inspirational and practical at the same time, it's another one of those must-have books for the shelf if you're interested in natural plant design.

An additional look into natural planting, especially if you're curious about native and nativar plants, is to read Doug Tallamy's *Nature's Best Hope* or the research by Dr. Annie White from the University of Vermont. They are leaders in the study of how cultivated selections affect pollinators.

A Year at Brandywine Cottage by David Culp was such an inspiring book for me as I built my own home landscape. He walks through each season of the garden, his favorite plants, and tells stories about the evolution of his space over the years. If you are looking for a list of plants and to see their practical application in David's garden, this is a wonderful addition to your library.

Similar to David's book, Floret Farm's *A Year in Flowers* shares Erin Benzakein's life on her cut flower farm, planting information, and design inspiration for making arrangements from the garden. While her scale is likely grander than you have at home (because who has the land for a massive cut flower garden?), she breaks down variety selection and creative details in a way that is so fun and engaging. And the photos are just spectacular; it's a great coffee table book in addition to the great information.

Brie Arthur is a fabulous speaker, author, and gardener who has built a career on teaching people how to blend traditional ornamental

gardening with foodscapes. She offers classes, books, and webinars to help you have success growing food in your garden just like you would any other ornamental plants. Both *The Foodscape Revolution* and *Gardening with Grains* give fantastic insight into creating these ornamental edible gardens in the home landscape.

Plant Partners: Science-Based Companion Planting Strategies for the Vegetable Garden by Jessica Walliser was an eye-opener for me. Jessica breaks down the science of what you plant next to each other in a relatable and inspiring way. If you're into maximizing what you can get out of your garden, this is a must.

Along the lines of edible planting, social media superstar Kevin Espiritu's book *Field Guide to Urban Gardening* is another amazing read, especially if you live in an urban environment or a home with limited outdoor space. He's got fun ideas and practical tools to maximize your edible output to keep your kitchen full.

Finally, one of my favorite garden writers of all time is the fabulous Margaret Roach, one of *The New York Times'* most beloved garden columnists. Her book, *A Way to Garden*, is her treatise on building gardening into a lifelong calling. It's beautifully written, beautifully photographed, and a treasure to read.

Now that you've gotten the gardening bug, I know that you'll want to keep going. My goal was to get you started, and my friends above will help keep you going. I hope that you enjoy their books as much as I have and hope that you are inspired to keep digging in the dirt. If you have others that you've read and want to share with others, be sure to tag me on Instagram @RyanPlantsPlants so I can share them with this *Field Guide* family and keep the conversation going. Have fun digging!

About the Author

Ryan McEnaney is a plantsman, designer, and communicator for all things green and gardening. He serves as a resource for, and has been seen in, *Real Simple*, *HGTV Magazine*, *Better Homes & Gardens*, *Martha Stewart Living*, *The Wall Street Journal*, and more. He has also appeared as an outdoor lifestyle and gardening expert on television and radio stations across the United States.

Ryan enjoys breaking down sometimes challenging gardening topics into relatable and digestible content. He travels the United States speaking at garden centers and other events to help people have success digging in the dirt and inspire them to think differently about gardening.

A fifth-generation family member and owner at Bailey Nurseries, one of the country's oldest and largest growers of shrubs and trees, he also serves as spokesperson for the company's consumer plant brands: Endless Summer® Hydrangeas, First Editions® Shrubs & Trees, and Easy Elegance® Roses. Along with this role, he hosts a digital series "Garden Gab" to continue his efforts of supporting home gardeners to have success with plants.

Based outside St. Paul, Minnesota, Ryan lives and gardens with his husband Paul and two dogs, Bear and Minny.

Photography Credits

Alamy, pages 27 and 141

Bailey Nurseries, pages 36, 54, 79, 114, 120, 124 (left), 128, 166 (middle), 167 (top, middle), 172 (top, middle), 174 (middle), 176 (top, bottom left), 180 (top), 183 (top), 184 (bottom left), 185 (middle, bottom right), and 186 (bottom), 208

Bushel & Berry, page 170 (bottom right)

Rob Cardillo, page 115 (top)

Joe Dodd (Linear Photography), pages 12, 40, 65, 81, 106, and 109

Carson Douglas (landscape design by), pages 12, 40, 65, 81, 106, 107, and 109

FASTILY, CC BY-SA 4.0, page 170 (middle)

JLY Gardens, pages 22–23, 45, 49, 58, 72–73, 86, 87 (right), 88, 99, 102–103, 111–112, 119 (left), 132, 145, and 165 (middle)

Martin Mann (Martin Mann Photography), page 107

Kelly Norris, pages 1, 14 (right), 52–53, 110, 173, 174 (bottom left, bottom right), 177 (top), and 181 (top, second from top)

Donald Pell, pages 33, 41, and 83

Proven Winners®, pages 167 (bottom right), 169 (bottom left), 170 (top, bottom left), 179 (top), 183 (bottom), and 185 (bottom left)

David Salman (High Country Gardens), page 180 (second from top)

Shutterstock, pages 13, 15 (right), 17 (top), 18, 20–21, 24, 37, 43, 55, 59, 69, 89, 113, 115 (bottom), 122, 130, 134, 143–144, 164, 171 (top, second from bottom, bottom), 172 (bottom left), 178 (bottom left), 179 (second from bottom), 180 (second from bottom, bottom), 181 (bottom), 182, 183 (second from top), 188 (top), 189 (middle), 190 (top), and 200

Forest & Kim Star, page 187 (bottom right)

Tracy Walsh, pages 4–6, 8, 10, 14 (left), 15 (left), 17 (bottom), 19, 26, 28–29, 32, 34–35, 38–39, 42, 46–48, 50–51, 57, 61, 62–64, 66, 68, 70–71, 74, 76–78, 80, 82, 84, 87 (left), 90, 92–97, 100, 104–105, 108, 116–118, 119 (right), 121, 123, 124 (right), 125, 127, 129, 136–140, 142, 149, 162, 165 (top, bottom left, bottom right), 168, 169 (top), 172 (bottom right), 174 (top), 175 (top, middle, bottom left), 176 (middle), 178 (top), 179 (second from top, bottom), 184 (top, middle, bottom right), 185 (top), 186 (top), 187 (middle, bottom left), 188 (middle, bottom left, bottom right), 190 (middle), and 202–203

Walters Gardens, Inc, pages 166 (top, bottom left, bottom right), 167 (bottom left), 169 (bottom right), 175 (bottom right), 176 (bottom right), 177 (middle, bottom left, bottom right), 181 (second from bottom), 183 (second from bottom), 187 (top), 189 (top, bottom left, bottom right), and 190 (bottom left, bottom right)

Wikimedia, pages 171 (second from top) and 178 (bottom right)

Adam Woodruff, pages 30–31, 60, and 131

Index

H

I

J

K

M

N

P